U-wun-ge-lay-ma

A Guide to Next-level Living

Dear David —

This book is about the
reach for Perfection — It
is a reach that I think we
are all meant to pursue —
I look forward to the Journey
with you .

Andrew L. Thorn, PhD

Library of Congress Control Number: 2010928399

Thorn, Andrew L.

U-wun-ge-lay-ma: A Guide to Next-level Living / by Andrew L. Thorn

ISBN 978-1-4276-5014-6

1. Next level   2. Success in life   3. Reaching for perfection

Cover design and illustrations by Raoul Ranoa

Telios Press books are available for special promotions, premiums, or corporate training. For details, contact Stacy Thorn, Special Markets, Telios Press @ 1-800-707-1864

First Paperback Edition - 2010

Dedication

I wrote this book for you . . .

Preface

U-wun-ge-lay-ma: A Guide to Next-level Living is an invitation to ponder your path to perfection. It is based on the idea that growth is more powerful than change, behaviors are more important than competencies, and questions are more valuable than answers. Perfection is possible and can be attained by anyone who dares to soar in ascending spirals. To reach for it, we must be willing to see it as a process.

Practice means to perform, over and over again, in the face of all obstacles, some act of vision, of faith, of desire. Practice is a means of inviting the perfection desired.

    Martha Graham

U-Wun-Ge-Lay-Ma • Andrew L. Thorn

Introduction

Success is a goal sought after by nearly every resident of our planet.

There are many books that are written with the hope of inspiring others to success. The majority of them are generally focused on the sciences of achievement and accomplishment.

Others are focused on the things we need to stop doing in order to become successful.

This book was written for successful people, those who have reached a comfortable place in their existence and are now trying to figure out "what's next." Specifically, it is written to those who want to reach for the next level and who know that, in doing so, they will eventually find themselves reaching for perfection.

They are not afraid of what they will discover on the pathways to perfection. They desire to become their best and are willing to become what they must become in order to enjoy a more enlightened way of living.

Each chapter ends with a section titled *"**Hearing Your Voice**."* The content of the chapter, the questions at the end, and the reflection exercises are written with one hope in mind: that you will listen to your own voice and record the personal wisdom you receive as you read this feeble attempt to describe the journey to the next level. Please listen to the inspiration you receive as you consider what it means to you to live at the next-level.

I recognize that, for many, the thought of reaching for perfection is absurd, but successful people know that, eventually, a life dedicated to continuous improvement will mold them into something very close to it. At that point, they will be the only ones who can reasonably detect what the next level looks like, because everybody else will see them as complete and fully developed.

Those who are reaching for something more will benefit the most from this book. Those who are looking for shortcuts to the next level will be greatly disappointed. We can accelerate our pace, but there are no shortcuts. The path begins with a dream, but you must be willing to become anxiously engaged in order to become your best.

Aim at perfection in everything, though in most things it is unattainable. However, they who aim at it, and persevere, will come much nearer to it than those whose laziness and despondency make them give it up as unattainable.

Lord Chesterfield

1

The Tale of the Name of the Tree

When I was a kid, the world was quite different than it is today. We didn't have cell phones, video games, iPods, or DVD players to steal away our creative moments. The lack of these technological wonders made it easy for us to hear our own voices.

Daily, we anxiously engaged in some project born out of our own imagination. When we finished one adventure, we quickly began another. All of our endeavors had one thing in common: they had to be better than the ones we did before.

Raising The Bar

I must admit, we tried a lot of harebrained schemes that never got off the ground, but, for some reason, we kept trying.

Taking things to the next level became second nature, but it was never easy. We always wanted to improve. We even dreamed that some of our inventions would get us listed in *The Guinness Book of World Records*. That was our constant quest. We wanted to get better.

One year, for Christmas, my sister and I received a record called *Danny Kaye Tells 6 Stories from Faraway Places.* One of the stories that particularly caught our imagination was called "The Tale of the Name of the Tree." This story originated with the people of Africa.

Danny Kaye had a knack for telling stories, and this one taught us that when we want to raise the bar, we must be willing to use all of our resources, even the ones that we generally overlook. It also taught us that the road to innovation and ingenuity is paved with unconventional wisdom. In other words, stretching to new heights sometimes requires us to act in ways that seem counterintuitive. To reach the next level, we must be willing to abandon what we know so that we can see things the way they really are, and as they really may be.

The Tale of the Name of the Tree

Over thirty years have passed since I first heard this story, and I am still affected by its message. I share this fable with you now as I begin this guide to the next level.

> There was, at this time, my friend, a great famine in the land. Now, in the land, there grew a great tree with fine fruit, but it was known that this fruit would only drop when someone spoke the name of the tree. So as the famine grew worse and worse, the people all came and lived near the tree, waiting for the fruit to ripen. When the fruit was almost ripe, it was found with dismay that no one knew the name of the tree!
>
> So they said, "Let us send the Hare to the Chief over the Mountains in order that he might tell us the name."
>
> The Hare accordingly set forth and soon reached the kraal of the Chief over the Mountains. When he asked the Chief for the name of the tree the Chief replied, "That

tree is called U-wun-ge-lay-ma. When you get back, stand beneath it and say 'U-wun-ge-lay-ma,' and the fruit will fall."

So the Hare hurried on his way back to his people. But he had not gone far on the path when he tripped over a root and rolled down the hill. And before he reached the bottom, the name of the tree had gone out of his head!

He tried all the names he knew and many others as he went along. He said, "Is it U-wun-tu-le-gay-le, or U-wayn-gay-le-tu-la, or what?" All the way, he tried to remember, but when he arrived at the tree, although he tried many words, not a piece of fruit fell!

Now the people said they would send the Springbok, for he was so swift he would return before he had forgotten the word. So the Springbok set out and arrived in no time. Then the Chief told him, "That tree is called U-wun-ge-lay-ma."

And he started back as fast as he could to return to his people. But in his haste, he tripped over an anthill, and before he could pick himself up, the name was gone! He tried all the names he knew on the way, but in vain. When he got back, all he could say was, "U-wun-ge-lay-tum-ba," and that was no use!

So the people said they would send the Kudu, for he was stronger and would not fall on the way. So the Kudu set out and soon arrived at the Chief's kraal. The Chief over the Mountains told him, "The name of that tree is U-wun-ge-lay-ma," and the Kudu thanked him and started back.

But on his way, he caught his horns in the branches of a tree. While he was freeing himself, he forgot to say the word, and it went out of his head! When he had freed himself, it was gone. And when he returned to his people, he had to admit that he had forgotten it.

The people now said they would send the Lion, for he was both swift and strong, and he had no horns to catch in trees. The Lion got the word from the Chief over the Mountains and started home, repeating the word to himself. But the sun was hot and he was tired. He lay down to rest in the shade of a bush. And he slept. But when he woke, the name was gone out of his head!

Now the Lion was too proud to admit he had forgotten the word, so he made up a word and said it many times to the tree. But no fruit fell. Then the people said, "Nonsense! There is no such word! You are no better than the others, for you have forgotten also." And they were very sad, for their hunger was growing and the fruit was ripening.

At last, the Elephant said, "Let us send the Tortoise." All the animals laughed, for they were sure no one so slow could remember.

But the Lion said, "Let him go. Since we have all failed, it is best that he should fail also."

But before the Tortoise left, he went to his mother and asked her, "How does one remember a very hard word?"

His mother said, "If you wish to remember it, do not stop saying it for any reason."

After a long time, the Tortoise reached the kraal of the Chief over the Mountains and the Chief told him, "The tree is called U-wun-ge-lay-ma." The Tortoise asked him again, and the Chief told him yet again. The Tortoise asked him a third time, and the Chief said the word yet again.

So then, he set out, saying the name to himself. When he came to the anthill, he said "U-wun-ge-lay-ma" as he went around it. When he came to the tree, he just went on saying it. And again, when he came to the bush, although he was very tired and it was very hot, he only said "U-wun-ge-lay-ma" and kept on.

At last, he reached his home, and his wife said, "You are very tired. Will you not rest?"

But the Tortoise said "U-wun-ge-lay-ma" and went on.

When he reached his friends underneath the tree, they all said, "What is the name? Tell us the name of the tree!"

And he said, "U-wun-ge-lay-ma."

And the fruit immediately began to fall. And the people ate and were hungry no longer, and they said, "We will make the Tortoise Chief over all the people, for he has brought us the name of the tree!"

And now, my friend, can you remember the name of that tree?

Hearing Your Own Voice

Before moving on to the next chapter, please re-read the fable. This time, consider your place in the story.

Where do you fit?

_____

_____

_____

Which character is most like you?

_____

_____

_____

How do you remember the important lessons of your life, so that they are fresh when you need them?

_____

_____

_____

You are not required to walk by memory. There is space at the end of each chapter to summarize your thoughts, but it is not enough to capture all of them. You may wish to purchase a companion journal to preserve your more prominent reflections and key learnings.

The journey to the next level will require you to develop a very introspective approach. If you really want to raise the bar, you must become comfortable examining your own way of being and documenting your findings. You must be willing to grow and develop.

T.S. Eliot described the journey to the next level this way:

> *"Only those who will risk going too far can possibly find out how far one can go."*

You are now free to be whoever you want to be!

2

Clearing the Way

If you have a good imagination, you may have seen yourself and others in this story. If you read it without applying it to yourself, then please take a moment and read it again with these two questions in mind: Which character in the story most resembles me? Which character would the people around me say that I am most like?

The majority of us see our self as the Tortoise, the hero of the story. We believe that we would remember the name, and we even tell ourselves that it is a simple name and wonder why anybody would forget it. We would have returned with the name, saved the people, and taken our rightful place as ruler of the world.

Stumbling Blocks

Even though this is a fairly unrealistic belief, it is quite common. Most of us can easily see the faults and shortcomings of others, but we have a much more difficult time identifying or owning up to our own. As a result, we are unable and/or unwilling to see the obstacles that may prevent us from reaching for the next level.

Consequently, some of the most successful people end up tripping on their own carelessness. Many never make it to the next level because they are blinded by their inability to see the truth about their own behavior, so they pass through life rationalizing their behavior and blaming others for their circumstances. This really does affect us all. Sometimes, like the Hare, we trip over the smallest obstacle and forget who we are. Then we think we can make something up. We truly believe that we can create a counterfeit "self" and that no one will notice. When we lie to ourselves enough times, we can no longer discern the truth. We show up, pretending to be something or someone that we are not. Even when our intentions are good, we are incapable of being authentic. We try so hard to make ourselves believe that we have the answer, but in the end, no fruit falls.

At other times, we are like the Kudu. We believe that our individual strengths will carry us through life even when we come up short. We think that our good looks, our fancy car, our million-dollar home, our physical strength, and our youth will shield us from paying the price when we fail.

Unlike the Hare and the Springbok, the Kudu never even tried to make up a name. He just went to the tree and admitted that he had forgotten the name. He knew he would face no consequences because he was the biggest and the strongest. Because of his superior strength and ability, nobody would dare call him a failure. He got a pass because nobody had enough courage to challenge him.

Most of us probably didn't think much about the Hare, the Springbok, or the Kudu. We understand their shortcomings. They seem minor, so we forgive them. Their reasons for forgetting seemed innocent enough, and we can imagine ourselves running into the same set of circumstances and facing the same problems. We just would have been more focused and remembered the name.

The Lion, on the other hand, seems to have no excuse, and it is very difficult for us to show him any sympathy. He forgot the name of the tree because he was too tired to continue on. He paused to take a nap, and when he awoke, he had forgotten the name.

When he got to the tree, he was too proud to admit he had forgotten it, and he insisted that he knew the name. He just kept repeating the word to the tree, hoping that the fruit would fall.

But that wasn't the worst thing that his pride caused him to do. His grandest form of denial was that he believed that since he couldn't get the job done, nobody could. When it was suggested that the Tortoise be sent, he said, "Let him go. Since we have all failed, it is best that he should fail also." The Lion never believed for a minute that the Tortoise might be successful. He assumed that since he had failed, everyone else would fail too. In his mind, nobody could be successful.

If you are normal, you might have thought something like this as you read about the Lion. "I know somebody just like that." Very few of us would ever think, "That sounds like something I would say or do." Yet most of us, at some point or another, have treated others in exactly the same way as the Lion treated the Tortoise.

Before we can effectively consider our journey to the next level, we must understand a significant problem. This problem is significant because it affects everyone, even the most successful of us. In order to conquer these impediments, we must be willing to look very deeply into our own behavior. Eliminating these traits is a difficult process, but success is not possible until we do.

Self-Deception

The inability to see our own faults combined with the ability to project those faults onto others is called self-deception. Self-deception is the process of denying or rationalizing away the relevant, significant, or important evidence that growth is needed in order to maintain forward progress. It generally results in blaming others for our problems instead of creating the development plan we need to grow and become our best selves. As a result, our growth is stymied.

Despite the hideous nature of self-deception, it is normal behavior. Each of us, in some way, is afflicted with this problem. We suffer greatly because of this affliction, yet we do very little to combat it. It touches every aspect of our life because it filters our experiences and keeps us from seeing things as they really are.

The reason we do so little about it is because we rarely know when we are doing it. The symptoms that we so easily detect in others are very difficult for the self to observe and detect. Each success we enjoy creates a false sense that all is well. Each time someone overlooks one of our faults, we tell ourselves that our faults don't matter. Self-deception dulls our ability to see our own faults and potential growth areas. This subtle decay creates blind spots that keep us from seeing the next steps in our own personal development.

There are two prominent forms of self-deception: that which we do consciously and that which we do unconsciously. They both prevent us from being our best. They are both detectable if we focus on the right questions. We may never be able to eliminate self-deception completely, but we can grow. All it really takes is a desire to become better and to move forward.

Conscious Self-deception

The conscious form of self-deception is most clearly demonstrated by the way we receive feedback from others. Many of us, when given true and accurate feedback, decide to defend against it instead of believe it and do something about it. This choice to defend our wrongedness and debate the people that have given us the gift of feedback limits our ability to grow and progress. The more we debate and defend it, the less interested those around us become in giving us future feedback, even when we need it most.

I call this a conscious form of self-deception because we usually know that the feedback we are receiving is true. Our hope is that we can convince everybody else that it is not true. We hope that others will not see our flaws or that we can convince them that they must be confused or that they didn't see us accurately if they do. A conscious choice is made to defend the behavior instead of correcting it.

We say something like, "If John really knew me, then he would not think that way about me." Or even, "This is the way I am, and if Tina doesn't want to accept who I am, then I don't care what she thinks."

This type of thinking prevents us from addressing the problem. We get lost in our excuses and reasons instead of solving the problem.

So how do you fix this problem?

The first step is to accept that John and/or Tina are right. This does not make you wrong. It just means that the feedback that they have given you is an accurate reflection of how they see you.

You may be right too. You may be very good at the behavior or competency that they are criticizing, but they have not seen you at your best. You simply have not demonstrated this skill to them yet.

The diagram below helps me illustrate this point. Let's assume that you interact regularly with John and he thinks you are a bad listener. Let's also assume that you possess terrific listening skills and that John doesn't really know you that well, even though he interacts with you often. This relationship can be diagramed in the following way:

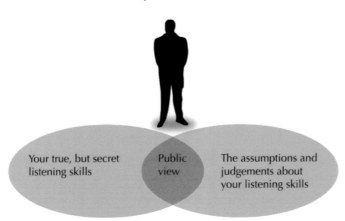

The only information available to John is what occurs in the intersection of this relationship diagram. This intersection represents the regular and frequent interactions that you have with John. Even though he only sees and hears what happens during these interactions, he later builds upon what he sees and hears by making judgments and assumptions to create meaning. The only information John has to go by is your behavior during each interaction.

If you behave poorly during these interactions, for whatever reason, then you have kept your true self out of the interaction and it remains a secret to John. He only sees what you put into the public domain.

The only way you can change what John thinks is to put more of your best self into the interactions you have with him. You have to widen his access and expand the zone.

We often fail to do this out of simple neglect. We think we can get by without stretching the zone, so we settle for that. Usually, we get by, because others are unwilling to confront us. This makes it easier for us to keep doing the same old, same old. We convince ourselves that there is no need to grow, that we don't have time to grow, and that nobody expects us to grow. Then we act surprised or hurt when we receive anonymous 360-degree feedback telling us that we have not grown or that we need to grow.

One of the most interesting things I discovered in giving feedback to over a thousand people is that each person always knows what the report is going to say before they see the report. I know they know, because I ask them what they think the findings will be before we look at their report. They tell me, and then when we look at their report, they are always right. They say that they have heard it before and often for a very long time.

This is why I call this conscious self-deception, because in almost every case, the person knows what others think and refuses to do anything about it. For some unknown reason, hope exists that they can keep on doing what they have always done without any concern or need to change. They figure that if they have gotten this far without changing, why would they have to change now? Thus, they deny themselves the opportunity to grow and improve.

Unconscious Self-Deception

All forms of self-deception keep us from seeing our own contribution to the problem, but the unconscious form is especially blinding. The Lion demonstrates this perfectly when he projects his own failures upon the Tortoise. He never legitimizes his own failures by admitting he failed. He simply shifts the focus to the Tortoise and equates slowness with a lack of power. He believes that the Tortoise will fail because he was not able to travel a great distance without forgetting the name of the tree. He believes that, just as he did, the Tortoise will tire, rest, and forget the name.

This is the most common form of unconscious self-deception. It is the keen ability each of us possesses to identify our own faults in others. When somebody we know, or even don't know, demonstrates one of our own faults, we are quick to judge and belittle them. When we do this, it takes the pressure off ourselves and places it safely onto somebody else. We don't have to look at what we are doing or who we are. We can just point our finger at others and condemn them for doing what we do.

It is difficult and painful to see our own faults and weaknesses. When we do, it knocks us down and makes us feel inadequate. Nobody likes to feel this way; it is unproductive and keeps us from becoming our best selves. It is also difficult to resolve these feelings, especially when we are unable or unwilling to do something about them.

The easiest way to avoid feeling this way, and to avoid doing anything about it, is to transfer our discomfort onto somebody else. When we notice one of our faults in somebody else, we no longer have to recognize it in ourselves.

Each of us truly dislikes, even hates, the faults and imperfections that encumber our own characters. Sometimes, despite our successes, these very faults can cause us to dislike, even hate, ourselves. The identification of these faults in others makes it possible for us to avoid this debilitating form of self-judgment.

I don't think I am unique in the behavior that I am describing, but I realize that I can only speak for myself. When I reflect upon the reasons why I dislike the people I do, I usually discover that it is because of some character flaw they possess. Upon deeper reflection, I find that I usually possess the same character flaw, and that this is a part of me that I do not like. Since I am most productive when I like myself, I am willing to do everything I can to push these feelings of dislike and inadequacy onto somebody else. In other words, I don't want to dislike or hate myself, so I dislike or hate somebody else for the very characteristics that I am unsatisfied with in myself.

Another blinding form of unconscious self-deception is the propensity to blame others for what happens to us. Our society is constantly confirming the idea that we are all victims and that somebody else is to blame. As a result, more and more people are becoming powerless to become their best self. They are being lulled by the idea that it is not their fault. Many people in our society now believe that they are owed something, and when they don't get it, they feel as if they have been cheated.

I am often engaged by organizations to develop and foster shared accountability. I am usually met enthusiastically by the people with whom I will work. They tell me that they are glad that we are finally going to do something about accountability because no one else is acting responsibly. The other guy is never doing enough, and the person I am talking to is often the victim of the other person's inability to be accountable.

What Is My Contribution to the Problem?

The way out of unconscious self-deception is actually very simple. The first step is to focus on a problem that needs to be solved. It doesn't matter what the problem is or where it is occurring. Just identify the problem, and then take a look at all of the people and circumstances that contribute to the problem.

After you have identified all of the key stakeholders in the problem, ask yourself, "What is my contribution to the problem?" As soon as you figure that out, forget about what everyone else is doing, and go to work on resolving your contribution. It is the only part that you can actually change. You can't change anybody else. They will have to change themselves.

Even if you own the smallest part of the problem, resolving that part will reduce the trouble the problem is causing. The illustration below helps me put it all in perspective. Some people own a larger percentage of the problem, but they still only own a part of the problem.

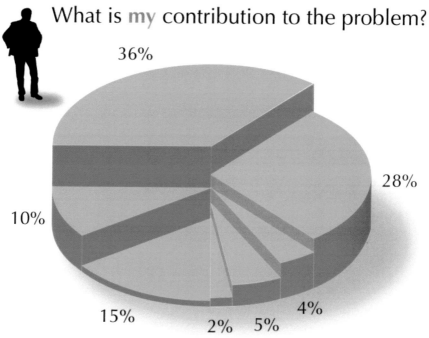

What is my contribution to the problem?

36%

28%

10%

15%

2%   5%

4%

Sometimes I own a large part of the problem, and sometimes I own a small part of the problem. Once I identify it, I have the power to do something about it. Once I focus on my contribution, I am free from the blame game, and I no longer feel like a victim. My power is restored, and I transition from a stagnant state to a growth spurt.

Hearing Your Voice

Before you continue on to the next chapter, I want you to try this exercise. Think of a problem that is currently challenging you. Think about all of the people who are involved in this problem and what they are doing to cause such trouble. Now include yourself in the mix and ask yourself about your own contribution to the problem. Ask yourself the following questions:

What is my contribution to the problem?

_____

_____

_____

How can I best contribute to the resolution of this problem?

_____

_____

_____

What behaviors or competencies do I need to develop in order to help resolve this problem?

_____

_____

_____

Do I hold myself fully accountable in work, or do I shift responsibility when things go wrong?

_____

_____

_____

Whom do I need to stop blaming?

_____

_____

_____

Am I open or closed to correction?

_____

_____

_____

How can I empower myself to grow in the ways necessary to resolve this problem?

_____

_____

_____

Who can help me grow?

_____

_____

_____

Carl Jung, the wise and great philosopher, once made the following statement.

> *"The greatest and most important problems of life are all fundamentally insoluble. They can never be solved but only outgrown."*

As I ponder this thought, I realize that the only real way to successfully overcome self-deceptive behavior is to understand that it is occurring and then develop a plan to grow and move beyond it.

> *U-wun-ge-lay-ma!*

3

Setting the Course

From the time we are born, we begin to reach for new heights. We want to walk. Then, we want to run, jump, skip, and sing. Inside each of us is the desire to grow and to become the best that we can be. Simply stated, we are born with a desire to be better.

We soon discover that growth can be painful and that excellence requires effort. The road to enlightenment is poorly lit and difficult to navigate. We hear the word "no" far more often then we hear the word "yes." The fatigue caused by living in a blurry and fast-paced world can diminish our tolerance for stretching ourselves. As a result, many seek an easier path.

An Unlevel Playing Field

There is much in this world that diverts attention and threatens an individual's opportunity to reach his/her true potential.

Unfortunately, some of our fellow travelers begin life in corrupt environments. Their growth is stunted by a lack of positive guidance. Only a small number ever break out to recognize personal greatness. Through no fault of their own, they experience limited opportunities to become great. Real chances to exit the maze and seek maximum development are few and far between. They spend their lives wanting, with almost no way to satisfy their desires.

Others find themselves in the richest of environments, yet somehow become distracted by the baubles, trinkets, and beads of the world. Their desire to grow and reach for higher development is suppressed by the dim light of their smallest success. The gluttony of their surroundings overcomes them, and they too fail to become all that they can be. While some find their way out, the majority of these people are satisfied with the status quo and never stretch to reach their full potential. They fail to stretch because there is no compelling reason to stretch. They face very few real challenges to their survival. Their only real objective is to find new ways to entertain themselves.

Dare To Dream

Some are afraid to dream. They find it very difficult to imagine becoming their personal best. They do not believe that the seeds of greatness are within them. They believe that others are destined to be great and that there is only room in this world for so many great people.

They haven't always thought this way. In their youth, they believed in their own uniqueness. They believed that they were special and that they would somehow rise to the top. Along the way, they faced the disappointment of being passed over and became discouraged. Each disenchanting experience knocked a little bit of their confidence away.

Maybe this has happened to you. Fortunately, it is a simple problem to fix. Yes, I said simple, but you must not confuse simple with easy. In order to fix this problem, you must be willing to examine your life every day and resolve to become just a little better. You must be willing to do whatever it takes to grow incrementally each and every day. You must be willing to forget about the past and focus on the future.

Reaching for Greatness

There are also those who think they are destined for greatness regardless of their circumstances. They are the dreamers, the overachievers, the focused, and the disciples of continuous improvement. Growth and learning are two of their most important values. They are constantly considering how they can become better than they have ever been. The world they dream of has no limitations. They are continually stretching themselves and looking for new ways to fly higher. It is rare that they are discouraged. The more they learn, the more they become aware that there is still so much to learn. They are always reaching, and good enough never is.

Those who travel this path sometimes tire and pause to rest before the next great adventure or stretch. It is rare that they become complacent on these plateaus of success, but sometimes they need a gentle push or a shove in order to climb the next mountain. The push can come from above or below. That push almost always comes at a time when it is more desirable to simply float in the current of past successes. It comes at a time when it would seem much more enjoyable to savor the view just a bit longer.

The Formula for Becoming Your Best

The formula for reaching the next level is the same for everyone. Even if you are the biggest dreamer in the world and believe that you are destined to become the ruler of the world, you must be passionate about creating and implementing your own personal development plan.

Being passionate means that the driving forces that prompt you to grow and develop come from within you. You know what you want, you know what you have to do to get it, and nothing is going to stop you from getting it. You walk with purpose.

None of your key stakeholders will insist that you become great. Some will even cheer when you fail.

Your organization will not force you to develop yourself. They are paying you to perform, and that is what they are going to manage. They have an interest in helping you become your best, but they are naturally focused on making a profit. This means that most of their investment in you will be focused on the competencies you need. Very little will be applied toward helping you develop the behaviors you need.

Even though your family and friends would like you to grow out of some behaviors, they will generally accept you the way you are. I must tell you a secret. They will only accept you the way you are until they can't stand it anymore, and then, they too will move on. They will not insist on your development. They simply hope and dream that you will wake up and develop yourself.

The same is true in every other circle of influence in your life. The anonymous aspiration of "if it is to be, it's up to me" must become your clarion call. You are the master of your individual development. You set the course. You decide if you are tired or if you are energetic. You decide if you stay or if you go.

Set Your Course

One of our major challenges is living in a world that demands speed. We don't just want it now; we want it twenty minutes ago. This focus sometimes leads us to believe that our competency is the most valuable commodity that we possess.

Your ability to perform is important, but it is not enough to sustain your forward progress in any aspect of your life, nor is it your most valuable commodity. You are your most valuable commodity, not the work you do. In order to be seen as a leader, you must maintain a persistent and continuous focus on your individual developmental objectives. Those who learn to improve their behavior never have a hard time finding work, even in the slowest of economies.

Sadly, you have probably noticed that the training and development budget is usually the first thing cut when times get tough. You may have also noticed that when you get busy, your development goals are usually the first thing that is abandoned. We tell ourselves that we will work on them later, but later is a myth. Nobody ever really has time for it.

Allowing yourself to focus on improving your competencies and your behaviors at the same time is not as tricky as it seems. It will, however, require you to adopt a new frame of reference.

Most people forget about the things that have the greatest amount of long-term impact. Some of these items may end up on our "To Do" list, but they usually end up not getting done due to what we believe to be more pressing matters. The things I am talking about don't necessarily take much time to do either; they just don't have to be done now, so we don't do them. They cause the least amount of immediate pain if we don't do them today, yet our failure to do them is what causes us the greatest amount of pain tomorrow.

The Quest for Killer Abs

There are many examples that I could use to illustrate this point. One of the most meaningful to me is one from my own life. When I was a teenager, I was quite athletic. I was never all-state anything, but I could play just about any sport. I was active, and I rarely felt any aches or pains from exercise. I believed that I would always be athletic.

As I moved into new life experiences, I did not create as many opportunities to be physically active. Despite my inactivity, I always considered myself an athlete and knew that I could compete if I would just take the time. I told myself that I would have time to do it when I finished this project or that project. I never felt unhealthy, nor did I gain that much weight. I looked like I was still in shape (at least I thought I did).

When my wife was about to turn thirty, I asked her what she wanted for her birthday. She said, "Killer abs." I was extremely excited and said as much. She said, "I am glad you are excited, because I don't want them on me. I want them on you."

I had always said that I could return to my high school shape with a mere two weeks of intense training. I could not have held a more wrong belief. Twelve years had passed by with very little exercise. I discovered very quickly that it was going to be a lot harder than I imagined.

What happened to me? Nothing different happened to me than what has happened to a lot of people. I failed to stay in shape. I failed to work out a mere thirty minutes a day, and this caused a severe decay in my physical abilities. I experienced sore muscles as I recreated my physical fitness.

Parts of my body hurt that had never hurt before. I was officially in trouble, and I had to work a lot harder than I ever would have had to if I had just consistently gone about keeping myself in good physical shape. From this, I learned that pain is a part of the journey. If we want to grow, we must learn to accept it.

The goal of "killer abs" was a lot more difficult than I imagined, and it took me more than ten years to reach it. Even though I passed through this very painful learning experience, I still find myself going through periods when my commitment to physical exercise is non-existent.

Wake Up!

The driving force behind this book is to inspire you to wake up. It was not written for most people. It was written for successful people who know that they can become something more.

You are responsible for becoming your best. You cannot wait for somebody else to do it for you. It doesn't matter if you come from one of the corrupt environments that I described earlier, if you are squandering true potential, or if you are simply pausing along your way to greatness. If you want to accelerate your growth and become your best self, then you must be willing to move your feet.

I welcome you as we join each other on this expedition to excellence. At times, I have found myself lost or distracted by the noise of the world. Like you, I share the goal of creating harmony in both my professional and personal life.

Hearing Your Own Voice

Here, at the starting line, I invite you to carefully examine your way of being. Please take this opportunity to seriously inspect the way you are living your life. As you ponder this brief self-assessment, ask yourself the following powerful questions:

Who am I?

_____

_____

_____

Am I getting what I want out of life?

_____

_____

_____

Who is responsible for making sure that I become my best?

_____

_____

_____

Who do I want to become this year? Who do I want to become over the course of the next five years? How about over the course of the rest of my life?

_____

_____

_____

How can I development my best qualities?

_____

_____

_____

What do I hear when the world is silent?

_____

_____

_____

What is my life calling me to become?

_____

_____

_____

As you ponder these questions, please pay close attention to what you think and feel. Your voice is more important than any other. As you listen to yourself, notice the questions that you are asking. They may be different from the ones anybody else is asking. They will fit you better. Be still, and listen. What you hear will be most valuable.

I have long enjoyed the following thought from the American author Oliver Wendell Holmes. With my apologies to him, I have taken the liberty of updating the language he used to make it more inclusive. I think if he had lived during our time, he probably would have said it this way.

> *"One may fulfill the object of his or her existence by asking a question he or she cannot answer and attempting a task he or she cannot achieve."*

4

Time to Grow

One of the most powerful questions I ask myself is, "Who do I want to become?" Whenever I am feeling lost, I consider this query, and I instantly find myself connecting with who I am and who I want to be.

Though this inquiry evokes powerful thoughts, it is not enough to merely think. If we truly want to become our best, we must be willing to move our feet. That means doing whatever it takes to get better, which generally involves changing our behavior and way of being.

This poses a fairly significant problem. Let's face it: no one likes to change, especially successful people. Sure, we say we like change, but for some reason, we resist it as much as we possibly can.

The only time we really like change is when we are acting as the change agents and inviting others to change. The change that we prescribe always tastes better than the change prescribed to us.

Right now, you may be thinking that you know people who fit this description, but **you** really do like change and **you** embrace it as often as it is presented to you. It is always easier to see the truth about things in others, but what I am saying is just as true for you as it is for me and everybody else.

Not convinced? Please take a few moments to consider the last time someone asked you to change or to do something that you didn't want to do. What were your reasons for not wanting to do what they asked?

Some of the most common reasons are:

- I didn't like what they asked me to do.

- I didn't know how to do what they asked.

- I didn't trust the person who asked.

- I didn't have time to do what they wanted me to do.

- I considered it, but it wasn't the best solution for me.

- If they had known me better, they wouldn't have asked me to do this. They would have just accepted me for who I am.

Whatever your reason, and however valid, your reasons and excuses were a direct manifestation of your resistance to the change the other person wanted you to make. Simply put, we don't like change. We like things to be consistent. We like to be accepted for who we are.

Reframing Change

Now comes the dilemma. Even though we don't like change, we understand how important it is. We know that in order to become our best, we need to change, but we still resist it. Submitting to needed change is extremely difficult. We want to change, but because pain is usually associated with change, we let our doubts and fears get in the way.

This is true, because change is most often presented in terms of what we need to stop doing. Let me say this in a different way—the majority of the feedback we receive is focused on the things that others think we need to shrink or minimize in order to become most effective.

In order to stop doing something, we must first be willing to admit that what we are doing is wrong. Ultimately, this means that we must admit that we are wrong. Naturally, when faced with this challenge, most of us seek to protect ourselves. Once our defenses are alerted, we dig in and inadvertently begin to resist the required or needed change.

Even the definition of change, to transform or convert, conveys a negative result. Very few of us want to be transformed or converted. We don't like it when someone tells us how we should be. We value choice and we want to discover and choose our own pathway to becoming our best.

For whatever reason, good or bad, change evokes these feelings. It is difficult to fight our nature and our learned resolve. Only a few of us can become self-actualized enough to embrace the changes we need to make. This is why we need to reframe our dialogue around change. If we really want to become our best, we must learn to frame change in its most positive light.

Growth vs. Change

There is a better word that we can use to describe what we really desire when we call for change. The word of which I speak is "growth." Growth is most simply defined as an increase by natural development. While many of us are resisting the idea of change, only a few of us resist the idea of growth. We want to grow. Our growth is a symbol of our individual maturity.

We are much more open to growth, which is precisely why it is more likely to occur. We understand that growth, like change is difficult to accomplish, but for some reason, we are more willing to pursue it.

Growth is almost always framed in terms of what we need to start doing. Instead of being told what will happen to us if we don't stop doing something, we are told how happy we will be, how much better we will feel, and how much more we will have when we grow.

We accept pain as a part of growth. In fact, we have developed affirmations to deal with the pain. Who among us has never heard the phrase, "no pain no gain"? We understand that we can't grow if we are protecting ourselves, so we let our defenses down and allow ourselves to receive the nourishment, even when it is painful, so that we can become our best.

The pain of change is brutal. We feel a much different kind of pain when we grow. Sore muscles actually challenge us to lean into the discomfort, because we know that we will feel better as we grow stronger. Change never breeds that certainty.

Growth looks a lot like change, but it is totally different. Change is externally motivated. Growth is internally motivated. Change wants us to be like somebody else. Growth calls us to become our very best.

Accelerating Growth

Growth takes time. Before we can discuss how to accelerate it, we must consider the question, "How do we grow?" While the specific methods may be different for each of us, the answer is the same. All growth occurs as a result of personal experience.

Arnold Schwarzenegger is reported to have said, "No one ever got muscles by watching me exercise." If we want to grow, then we must quickly realize that the development of any competency or behavior is the result of experience in exercising that skill or behavior. We cannot expect it to happen any other way; there are no shortcuts.

The magnitude of our willingness to do is the chief indicator of our growth. Our desire to be anxiously engaged propels us beyond thinking and dreaming, deep into doing and being. There is no substitute for experience. It is the source of all knowledge. The way we feel in the midst of our life experiences provides us with the evidence we need to determine the worthiness of our growth objectives. If we feel miserable, then we know we are pursuing an inappropriate goal. If we feel terrific, we know we are on to something good. It is that simple.

To accelerate our growth, we must learn how to accelerate our individual and personal experiences. Each day, we choose how we spend our time. We cannot expect to learn how to sing if we spend our time playing golf. We cannot expect to become proficient at math if we study English. Our activities must be aligned with the competencies and behaviors we desire to develop.

The mistake most of us make is in believing that we cannot accelerate our experience. We believe that experience is time bound. We fail to realize that time, by itself means nothing. In other words, the only thing I can say for certain about this time next year is that I will be either dead or alive. The way I use the time in between now and then is entirely up to me. We choose how we spend our time and we get what we put into it. Our commitments define our progress.

Consider two people learning to play the guitar. One person is committed to practicing thirty minutes a day, and the other is committed to practicing eight hours a day. At the end of one week, there is a noticeable difference between the two guitar players. One is remarkably more proficient than the other. The same week has passed for both, but the person practicing only thirty minutes a day would have to practice for sixteen weeks before he had the same experience of the person practicing eight hours a day.

The determining factor of growth is the rate at which we practice what we want to improve. It is possible to produce results normally seen over a long period of time in a very short period of time. All we have to do is choose how we are going to spend our time. This is the secret of taking things to the next level. If you want to reduce the time required for you to become your best, then you must be willing to accelerate the experiences that lead to your development. There is no need to wait for the years to pass; simply increase the frequency with which you engage in the behavior, and your rate of improvement will increase.

Behaviors can only be grown through experiences. If you want to become your best, then you must be willing to work on becoming your best all the time. You must be willing to engage others and learn from their perspectives. You must be willing to step forward and raise the bar. It is only when we apply what we learn that we become who we want to become.

Hearing Your Voice

Ponder the following questions carefully, and engage yourself in the reflective exercises. As you do, you will begin to see things as they really are.

Who do I want to be when I grow whole?

_____

_____

_____

What behaviors and competencies do I need to develop to become that person?

_____

_____

_____

What are my primary strengths? How developed are they?

_____

_____

_____

What experiences will help me accelerate my desired growth?

_____

_____

_____

Identify a behavior or competency that you want to develop. Complete the following sentence:

"When I get better at _____, I will _____(fill in the blanks by mentioning your growth area and one benefit that will result from your improvement in this area).

Repeat this process at least ten times, each time coming up with a new benefit. Listen closely to your inner voice as you recite these potential benefits.

Do these benefits inspire you?

_____

_____

_____

Do they fill you with a desire to engage in the activities that will bring about this growth?

_____

_____

_____

Do you believe that growth in this area will be meaningful to you?

_____

_____

_____

Only proceed with your development plan if you can see the benefits. Your time is valuable. Don't waste it on the development of behaviors or competencies that don't inspire you. You will only be able to sustain the activity necessary for growth in those areas that truly motivate you to be better.

Growth is a simple goal to achieve. All you have to do is experience it.

Confucius said, *"I hear and I forget. I see and I remember. I do and I understand."*

Time to get moving!

5

Sustaining Growth

Most us have attended a development seminar, read a great motivational book, or listened to an inspiring speaker. I call those experiences "igniting moments." They have the power to fire us up, but the flame generally burns out before we accomplish any real growth. What sounds good in the moment becomes difficult to implement when we return to life.

I do not wish to discredit these types of experiences; I simply desire to frame them in their proper perspective. They cannot sustain us by themselves, nor are they meant for that purpose. They truly are designed to light our fire, but we must be the keeper of the flame.

The power of these experiences is extinguished when the seminar ends, the book is closed, and the speaker concludes. When it is over, the only voice that matters is your own. You are the one who decides how you implement what you learned.

Successful people understand this concept. Instead of just listening to what is being said, they are actively engaged in capturing the thoughts that are being stimulated. They turn things around in their own heads until it fits their needs and circumstances. Then they put themselves in motion. If something doesn't work, they try something else until they figure it out. They take the spark and use it to build their own fire.

Life Is Busy

Continuous improvement is not for the faint of heart. Just living at the speed of life can be very overwhelming. There are a few aliens among us who are able to constantly focus on growth and development, but the rest of us mere mortals find it difficult to sustain.

There are many misconceptions about accomplishment. One of the most common is the thought that extraordinary achievements are produced by people who rarely experience the normal problems and challenges of life. This couldn't be further from the truth. Those who we raise up as exemplars face just as many discouraging moments as everybody else on the planet. The big difference is that they know how to manage the ups and downs. Instead of becoming upset and frustrated when the going gets tough, they become focused and engaged. They never spend any time asking, "Why did this happen to me?" Instead, they ask, "What am I going to do now?"

When the moment of trial inevitably appears, they are able to rely on this focus because they previously spent a lot of time thinking about and living with their future in mind. They see what they want, and they identify what it will take to get there. In their visioning exercises, they already considered the potential obstacles and what they would do to overcome them. They are not surprised when they meet them. Instead, they are prepared and know exactly what to do. They view every setback as minor because they know what the big picture looks like and they understand that these complications are part of the plan.

Because they are so connected to the future, they create systems to ensure that their daily efforts are aligned with their future targets.

When things get busy, they have a plan to guide them. They rarely get off track, but when they do, they have their plan to bring them back in line.

Daily Questions

Staying focused is tough, no matter how successful you become. There is great value in having frequent reminders of the things that are most important to us. Life is full of competing influences and if we want to succeed, we must find a way to frequently remind ourselves of what matters most. Technological advancements are creating wonderful tools for us to use, but nothing beats the impact of another human being checking in and supporting our progress.

Marshall Goldsmith is famous for his thought leadership skills. He spends his days helping some of the most successful business leaders of our time become even more successful. Over the course of an eighteen-month period, I was privileged to serve as Marshall's personal coach. It was an amazing and wonderful experience.

Marshall is an extremely busy individual, and he is on the road for weeks at a time. This makes it difficult for him to stay focused. He needed a constant, something that he could rely on to stay on track. He tried many strategies before he hired me as his coach.

The basis of our engagement relied upon a process I developed called "Daily Questions." This meant that our interactions did not happen monthly or weekly; instead, we spoke every day. Every evening, at 10:00 PM, I called Marshall to check-in. We reviewed his behavior for the day, and he reported his progress on his goals.

He was responsible for creating the questions and making sure they were aligned with his long-term vision. I was responsible for calling, asking the questions, and tracking his responses. No negative feedback was allowed; I could only make positive, reinforcing comments about his efforts.

One of the questions I asked Marshall was focused on the amount of time he spent writing. At the time, he was in the process of writing his bestseller, *What Got You Here, Won't Get You There*, and his travel schedule made it difficult for him to write consistently. He credits this process for helping him to finish his book and to live a happier life.

Here is how he describes the experience in his own words:

> *"In spite of all my blessings, I can still sometimes get caught up in the day-to-day stress and forget how lucky I am.*

> *"Why does this process work so well? For one, it forces me to confront how I actually live my values every single day. I either believe that something matters or I don't. If I believe it, I can put it on the list and do it! If I really don't want to do it, I can face reality, quit kidding myself, and take it off my list.*

> *"I asked my wife Lyda (also a psychologist) if she thought this process would work as well with a computer-generated list of questions instead of a live person. She said, 'No, it is a lot easier to blow off a computer than a friend.'"*

Marshall and I averaged about six and a half minutes per call. Some calls lasted only ninety seconds, and others, when time permitted, lasted much longer. The results of my "Daily Question" process were not attributed to the time we spent together. They can only be attributed to the frequency of asking the questions. Marshall knew I was going to call him each day, so he worked to be able to report positive results. Knowing that I was going to call him at 10:00 PM and that he was going to have to report on his day and answer for his actions served as a strong motivation.

Over the past twenty years, I have employed this process with many of my clients. It is a living process and one that easily focuses and breathes life into the successes of others. The results are profound.

Hearing Your Voice

Before moving on to the next chapter, consider the following questions and reflection exercise. You can only get from this chapter what you take out of it. Now is the time to capture your thoughts and discoveries. Do it before they fade away!

Am I willing to do what it takes to grow?

_____

_____

_____

How will I make sure that I will not be too busy to grow?

_____

_____

_____

What will be my constant?

_____

_____

_____

What am I willing to do to ensure that I never let another one of my brilliant thoughts escape? How will I record and implement them into my daily life?

_____

_____

_____

What strengths can I use to support my growth?

_____

_____

_____

Whom can I enroll to help me?

_____

_____

Imagine a friend of yours is going to call you every night and ask you questions about your life. What questions would you want this person to ask?

_____

_____

_____

_____

Write the questions that you want your friend to ask. Even the process of writing the questions will help you better understand your own values and how you can become your best.

_____

_____

_____

_____

Be courageous. Recruit a friend, and start asking these daily questions to each other. Keep a journal of your results.

The call to become great offers us something very different from change. It offers us the opportunity to grow. Growth is not a given; it is earned by those who pursue it relentlessly. Where do you stand?

Success is not the result of spontaneous combustion. You must set yourself on fire.

Reggie Leach

6

The Ladder of Success

As a young man, I embarked on a career in sales. I was fortunate enough to be surrounded by some pretty savvy sales experts. They cared about me, and they became interested in helping me figure out how to be successful. I followed the training and counsel they gave me, and I enjoyed success.

At the time, I remember thinking about my successes and wondering if I could sustain them. I also remember worrying if I could ever "outdo" them, or if I would be one of those people who would look back and say, "I peaked early in life, and after that, it was all downhill."

Now, when I look back at those successes, I realize how truly insignificant they were, especially when compared to some of my other life successes. I don't share this to boast or brag. I am simply pointing out that for much of my life, I have been blessed to feel successful.

I don't think I am unique in this feeling. In fact, I believe that this is a characteristic that all successful people possess. They see themselves as successful before anybody else sees it. They recognize each success, no matter how small, and they quickly learn how to build on it.

It is nearly impossible to be successful if you can't see yourself being successful. If you don't believe it, who will?

When successful people look back on their successes, they see a pattern. They notice that each success became the foundation of the ensuing successes that they enjoyed. They generally feel successful, but rarely do they say, "I am a success!"

The older I get, the more clearly I begin to see that success is a state of mind. As I climb the ladder of success, I am grateful for each rung, but I understand that all of my successes are merely stepping-stones to the future me.

I am certain that this is a common characteristic of successful people. Because we have succeeded before, we believe that we will succeed in the future. We know that success is a continuous process, never to be finished. In fact, the joy is in reaching for a new success each day.

Who Am I?

One of the most powerful questions we can ever ask ourselves is the question, "Who am I?" Thinking of our many unique qualities as we answer provokes individual awareness in a way few other questions can.

Because of the complexity of the question, many fail to gain clarity of thought, yet this is a question that must be answered if we are to reach for our ultimate success, even our true potential.

For many, the answer to this question is a synopsis of what they do. This answer, by itself, can never inspire. While it is true that what we do is a part of who we are, the real answer is much deeper than that.

We Define Our Success

When I was in graduate school, I formed a wonderful relationship with a very successful leader. This relationship provided me with many exciting learning opportunities. I benefited immensely from the opportunity to work regularly with this individual. I know that I also brought value to him, but I can't help but think about and feel thankful for the many ways in which our association enriched my life.

I will never forget how our relationship began. One of my professors encouraged me to contact him. Since he lived close to the university, I sent him an email requesting a face-to-face meeting. I fully expected that he would agree, and I waited for his response. After a couple of email exchanges, we agreed upon a time to meet.

A few days before our meeting I received a call from his office. His assistant asked if I would please send over my resume so that this leader could review it before we met. This seemed like an odd request, especially since I was not looking for a job, but I agreed.

We met in his home, which happened to be in one of the wealthiest areas in the United States. Upon entering, I was ushered to a seat at his beautiful dining room table. The table was perfectly clean. There was only one object on it, my resume, and it was neatly positioned at the head of the table. I was seated and informed that my new friend would shortly arrive.

I must admit that I felt a bit intimidated by the room. As I inspected the beauty of it and the rest of this house, it was clear that this person enjoyed success at a level that I had rarely seen. As I sat quietly, I wondered about what I was in for.

In a moment, my friend entered the room. He did not enter in a usual way. Instead, he entered singing, "Rhinestone Cowboy," an old

Glen Campbell song. He took his chair, pulled it real close to mine, put his hands on my knees, looked into my eyes, and said, "Hello, I am_____. I am most famous for being_____. What are you famous for?" He then put out his hand for me to shake.

What Would You Say?

Before you read my response, I want you to ponder how you would answer this question. At once, it is both a powerful statement and a powerful question. How would you answer it? What would you say?

Do you think a question like this can be answered if you have never recognized and appreciated your individual successes? Can you answer a question like this if you have not considered what makes you unique? This was definitely the most incredible "who am I?" moment that I had ever faced. How would you respond if you found yourself in the same situation?

In that moment, I relied on all of my previous successes. Instead of feeling intimidated by this question, I felt confident. I don't recall ever really contemplating what I was famous for prior to this moment, but my answer flowed easily from me. I said, "I am Andrew Thorn, and I am famous for being the father of five beautiful children."

My simple and unassuming response caught him off guard. He said he had never heard an answer like that before. We came together in that moment in a way that I think would not have been possible had I answered any other way. That moment prepared us for the conversations that followed and the work we did together. We built a friendship on our love for remembering and valuing our families while we strived to be our best. We both understood that none of our worldly successes could compensate for a failure to be our best in our private lives. This mutual understanding bonded us together.

We Define Success

You and I get to define success. We are free to define it any way we want, and I am certain that the definition we create will ultimately be what we get. Not all successes are of equal value. This is why we must carefully consider how we will define it. Since we always get what we focus on, we must make sure that we are reaching for what matters most to us, or else our successes will feel vacant and hollow.

You are a success and I am writing this book for you. It is my belief that no matter where you find yourself on the ladder of success, you believe things can be better. You feel happy, and you want more. There is nothing wrong with that. We are meant to be creatures of eternal progression.

If you are really reaching for that goal, then you must continually be willing to polish and refine what success means to you. The more you experience, the more clearly you will see what is important. The more you see, the sharper your focus must be. This is the only way to truly reach for a life greater than the one you presently enjoy.

Happy New You

Your journey to the next level depends upon your ability to discover and rediscover the real you. It is a simple process that begins with an examination of what you value most. Your values reflect who you really are, and they rarely change.

As we grow, we gain a better understanding of what they mean and how they apply to our lives. This makes it possible for us to refine our actions and behaviors.

The first time I reflected on how I was spending my time, I was completely surprised to discover that I was engaged in a lot of activities that were completely misaligned with what I said I valued most. I think I was compromising because I was young and trying to make my mark on life. I was agreeing to do many things because I thought it was what I had to do in order to reach a point where I could live my life the way I wanted. I did this at the cost of being the authentic me.

I always told myself that someday soon, I would reach my vision of success, and then I would be able to live according to what I value most. This is one of the most debilitating stories we tell ourselves, because someday never comes. It is a story that robs us of our initiative to see things as they really are and as they really will be.

Live Today! Love Today!

I had a friend who was dying of lung cancer, and he impressed upon me the thought that I must wake up and live my life the way I knew I wanted to live it. He told me to never wait for someday again. He said successful people don't wait for someday. Instead, they live every day in success.

I didn't want to wait for my own "Last Lecture" experience to make this happen. I wanted to live my life according to my values, and I began to believe that I did not have to settle for anything less. I was unwilling to compromise any longer.

I asked myself, "What competencies and behaviors do I need to develop so that my life will be aligned with my values?" "How do I need to grow and who can help me do it?"

These questions inspired me to write three self-focusing questions that I committed to ask myself every day. As I grew toward my goal of living according to my values, I reviewed these questions and regularly changed them so that they were aligned with my new circumstances.

Looking back, the results are amazing, but I must clearly state that the growth is incremental. My vision of who I am is much clearer today than it was twenty years ago, because I have constantly focused on discovering what I can do to become my very best. I still have a long way to go, but I am on the trail and making good progress. This brings me great satisfaction and balance in my life.

As I mentioned earlier, the "who am I?" question is a tough one to answer. I sat in an existential psychology class and we grappled with this question for over three hours with very few answers. If we don't take the time to understand who we are, we drastically diminish our ability to become the person we desire to become. Without such self-examination, our opportunity to reach for our full potential is significantly limited.

Hearing Your Voice

It is time for you to listen to your own voice. I want you to listen to the real you—the you who is not fooled by what you do every day to survive or the image that others have of you, the you who wants more, the you who is energized by the thought of becoming your very best.

Wake up! It is time to clarify who you are and who you want to become. Yes, you are successful, but now it is time to reach for the new you. You have an opportunity to ask yourself questions every day that will help you reach for your best and raise your own personal bar.

I dare you to consider and answer the following questions. They are life-giving questions. They will breathe life into the new you.

What is your definition of success?

_____

_____

_____

What are your unique qualities?

_____

_____

_____

How can you spend more time using them to create a better you?

_____

_____

_____

What questions will serve as daily focusers for you to take your life to the next level?

_____

_____

_____

How do you need to live in order to be the authentic you every day?

_____

_____

_____

Imagine that you are visiting with a friendly sage. During the course of the conversation, you are told that in exactly one year, your time on this planet will be finished. There is no sadness, only joy. A vision of what may come next is opened to you. You are excited about your potential. You receive two warnings:

1. *You must use your time wisely. If you waste it, your future will not be as glorious as you saw in the vision.*
2. *You must not tell anybody about your fast-approaching death.*

You leave this meeting in a very energetic mood. You realize that time is short and that you must get to work. The following questions enter your heart, and you begin to anxiously create your plan.

1. *How do I define success? What does it look like?*
2. *How will I spend my time?*
3. *With whom will I spend it?*
4. *How will I make sure that I stay focused on the things that matter most?*
5. *What must I start doing today to ensure my success?*

Please share your answers with those closest to you. ***They are waiting to experience the real you.***

Of course, the above exercise is make-believe, but it is also very real. The truth is that your time is limited.

You can no longer afford to define your success by the amount of money you make. You must no longer settle; you are dying. Live every moment. It is worth it. Wake up!

As you strive to become your very best, I have one promise for you:

You ain't seen nothin yet!

7

The Next Level

We have a daughter who did not show an early interest in learning how to ride a bicycle. When she was nine years old, she asked Santa to bring her one. On Christmas morning, she was not disappointed. There, to her delight, was a beautiful, new purple bike.

She was excited to learn, so after all the gifts were opened, we went outside to go for a ride. The wobbly sensation made her feel afraid. After only a moment, she said she was done and that she did not want to try anymore.

We went inside, and a few minutes later, she wanted to go outside and try again. Together, we went into the front yard. I held the back of the bike and she pedaled. It still frightened her, so we took another break.

During that day, she got on her bike several more times. Each time, she gained a little more confidence until she finally mastered the process. When I knew her confidence was established, I let go, and she rode by herself.

First, she learned to ride straight, then, she learned to turn, then, she learned to stand up while riding, and finally, she learned how to stop. Of course, along the way, she fell down several times, but the joy of riding the bike by herself motivated her to get up each time.

I will never forget the smile on her face or the sound of her laughter when she felt safe and successful in her efforts. It was a great day to be her dad.

Common Competencies

A few days later, we left the neighborhood to go on a longer ride. It was clear that she enjoyed this experience, but the look on her face was much different. It no longer brimmed with utter excitement. In just a short period of time, the experience of riding a bike had become common.

As I thought about this, I realized that this is true for every competency we develop, even the most exciting ones. At first, the challenge is to learn how to do it, but once we master the skill, it becomes ordinary to us.

Do you remember learning how to drive a car? It was one of the most exciting times of life. Our focus was intense; we really had to pay attention to what we were doing. Now, when we get home, we barely remember if we stopped at that stop sign along our normal route. We know we did, but we are so comfortable driving that we often find ourselves safely thinking about other things when we are on the road.

The same thing happened when we learned to read. At first, we paid attention to every single word. Now we can read a whole article without seeing any of the words.

The Foundation of Success

Success begins with learning and developing competencies. They are the foundation for all that we do, but once the house is built, who really thinks about the foundation? We know it is there, but it is out of sight and out of mind.

The competencies we develop are the mark of our early successes, but after we become successful, they become less important. As soon as they become second nature to us, they move out of our awareness and into a subconscious realm. This is why we often hear, "It's just like riding a bike." Once we learn how, we rarely ever forget.

Next-level Development

New employees and young leaders are expected to develop the competencies they need to meet the demands of their jobs, but this focus clearly diminishes as a leader matures. That's because, eventually, one either becomes or fails to become competent. Once they have been trained for the job, there is little left to do besides the job itself. There is, however, a way to progress, and that progression is always associated with our behavior. If competencies make up the foundation, behaviors are the attractive features that distinguish one home from another.

The behaviors we develop set us apart and establish us as leaders. They move us from good to great to outstanding. As we become more attentive to developing individual behaviors, others see us as more successful.

More Evidence

Consider a marathon. By definition, it is a contest of greater than normal length requiring exceptional endurance. Those who wish to run a marathon must train enough so that they can run, dance, walk, or crawl 26.2 miles. The distance is the same for everybody. It doesn't matter how you do it, but if you want to be successful, you must cover the distance.

Most people who train and run in marathons do it with only one goal in mind: they just want to make it to the finish line.

Some, however, see it as a race. They train much differently than those who train to finish. They work harder, they endure more, and they constantly push themselves to give just a little bit more. They are not satisfied with merely finishing; they want to win.

Those who approach the race from a finisher's perspective salute and congratulate other finishers by saying "How did you do?" Those who approach it from a winner's perspective ask, "What was your time?"

Distance, in this case, is the competency. You cannot call yourself a finisher if you do not go the distance. The length of the course does not change from one marathon to the next. It is constant; no one can run less or more. If you want to run a marathon, you must run 26.2 miles. The distance run does not distinguish one runner from another. Every finisher is the same.

Speed is the behavior that sets the runners apart. The speed is the only thing that the contestants can change about the race. They may not be able to run more or less, but they can run faster or slower.

Competencies vs. Behaviors

As we reach for excellence, we realize that the possession of key competencies is a non-factor. I am not stating that they are unimportant; I am simply saying that they become common. Even the most ordinary leaders are expected to possess them. They are entry-level requirements for senior leadership roles. If you don't possess them, you are not getting in.

The law of success clearly dictates that success can only be achieved by developing the competencies upon which the specific success you are seeking is predicated. Simply stated, competencies are the common requirements. You can't be successful without them.

Successful people already know this. They know because they spent the time required to become competent, and they continue to reap the rewards.

At some point, they realize the fundamental nature of developing competencies and ask, "What else is there?" They want more, but they realize that becoming more competent won't offer any further competitive advantage.

At that moment, they begin to wonder how to take things to the next level. There are very few clues, especially since the training they receive is almost always focused on becoming more competent. They want more, so they invest in more training, but a return on their investment is rarely realized. They attend with the expectation that they will learn new things, only to discover the "same old, same old," so they think about last night's game or head out to the golf course.

As they move up the ladder of organizational success, they realize fewer and fewer training opportunities. They continue to look outward, but eventually, the very best look inward. For the first time, they recognize that the only thing they can change is their individual behavior. In that moment, they begin to understand the real issue.

This awareness leads them to see that their behavior is directly related to their ability to effectively lead others. Not only is it related to their ability to lead others, it is also related to their ability to befriend others, love others, and serve others. In a moment of clarity, they recognize that they will never run out of growth opportunities. Behavior is the growth area that must be conquered on a continual basis. No one is exempt.

Once one behavior is mastered, a next level behavior appears. The person who is willing to examine his or her life more deeply and push for greater self-awareness will always discover more and more behaviors to develop. There is no limit; the improvement cycle is continuous. This is what makes reaching for the next level possible.

The development of behaviors is not like riding a bike, driving a car, or reading a book. Behaviors are more like habits. They can be learned and unlearned. The trick is figuring out which ones we need so that we become our most effective selves.

Leveraging the Perspectives of Others

Developing our most meaningful behaviors is difficult to do in a vacuum. To be effective, we need to give our stakeholders a stake and invite them to help us. Those who benefit or suffer from our behaviors are in the best position to assist in identifying strategies for improvement as well as providing the mechanism for measuring our growth. These subjective "judges" can only help us if we let them.

Successful people approach their stakeholders differently than those who are just starting out on the path. They recognize that people already view them as successful, so they don't waste time seeking negative feedback. I know this sounds unconventional, but they really don't need it. They already know how to use it; that is how they became successful.

To move to the next level, they need to understand how to seek positive feedback. The road ahead is short. They need more frequent support for the goal, because they have already come a long way and they are tired and bored. They need a vision of how they can become better, not a critique of how they have done. They need people who will breathe life into their aspirations and dreams.

As they enroll their stakeholders, they must clearly state that they are looking for positive, forward-looking statements that will help them become better. They must remember to invoke the rule of "no negative feedback" and focus all suggestions for improvement in the form of encouragement. The finish line is near; now is the time to be cheered on. Any other voice is unacceptable.

Reaching for Greatness

To truly reach for greatness, one must eliminate all sources of toxic input. Success is achieved by letting go of fear and self-doubt. These uncertain feelings can only drive us so far. To really soar, we must eliminate our own toxicity. You climbed to the level you are at now by doing that.

For some reason, those on the brink of success hang on to toxic stakeholders, thinking that their negative perspective will keep them from living in the world of "little miss sunshine." Nothing could be further from the truth.

In order to be our best, we must free ourselves from all toxic advisors. Their poisons prevent us from reaching higher. We don't need their constant reminders of past and present failures. Our history reminds us that we have grown past them.

Instead, we need people who can see our light and encourage us to shine it brighter. I love being around people who permit me to shine my light. I am not fooled into believing that they do not see my weaknesses. I am sure they do, but their encouragement allows me to focus on spending my time on the things that I do best. The more time I spend on being my best, the less time I have to be anything less.

You can't develop yourself without the input of others, but you must be careful in selecting those who will help you. Imagine if I yelled at my daughter when she was learning to ride her bike, "You are always scared! You will never learn how to ride!" Do you think she would have ever learned to ride? Like mom always said, choose your friends carefully. Make sure they are breathing life into your dreams.

Hearing Your Voice

By now, you know the drill. This chapter will not be complete until you pause to consider what is going on inside your head. There is no need to hurry to the next chapter. It will still be there when you finish.

What behaviors will move you from good to great to outstanding?

_____

_____

_____

What marathons are you running? How can you work harder, endure more, and push yourself to be more?

_____

_____

_____

Are you focused on developing competencies or behaviors?

_____

_____

_____

What is the next level for you?

_____

_____

_____

We really need to be looking beyond the next level. When we do, we reach the next level with little or no effort. This is because when we reach for something far beyond our normal capacity, the next level is easy.

Consider the behaviors that you desire to develop. Create a list of these behaviors. After careful consideration, pick the one that will be most meaningful to you to develop.

Now think of all the people who influence your life and who are in a regular position to witness your efforts for improving this behavior. Write down the names of these people.

Which of these people do you trust to breathe life into your development?

Call the people you trust and ask them to help you. Let them know why you selected them. Tell them that you would like a regular opportunity to received positive, forward-looking suggestions from their perspective. Offer to do the same for them.

Don't worry if this exercise scares you or if it feels awkward. Remember that the wobbly feeling of riding the bike frightened my daughter, but because she stuck with it, she overcame her fear. The same will happen to you.

There is nothing with which every person is so afraid as getting to know how enormously much s/he is capable of doing and becoming.

Soren Kierkegaard

8

Pathways of Perfection

I am fascinated by a phenomenon that I call "the last five pounds." Anybody who has ever been on a weight loss campaign understands this without much explanation. In the beginning, our efforts yield what looks like immense progress, but there comes a point when we feel like we are at a complete standstill. The major gains we once enjoyed are now barely recognizable. Maintenance is a difficult proposition in and of itself, and when we get close to realizing a soul-stretching goal, the remaining distance can appear next to impossible. Many have come within five pounds of their ideal weight, only to discover that the "last five pounds" can seem like the impossible dream. It is here, like the Lion from *The Tale of the Name of the Tree*, that many pause to rest.

This is what is known as a success plateau. From this vantage point, we can see our goal, but the path now looks much steeper and more difficult than ever. It takes a lot of effort to keep going, but that is exactly what we must do.

As we look ahead, we realize that what used to be good enough will no longer serve us now. After a while, we realize that the journey to the next level is really a journey to perfection. The fact that most of us are far from perfect does not mean that we cannot reach for perfection, but for some reason, many successful people are afraid to state the goal. They think that others will see them as cocky or arrogant if they say, "I am reaching for perfection."

Some turn back at this point because they think it can't be done. They have learned that "nobody is perfect," and they believe it. It is possible, and in order for us to go for it, we need to begin to understand what perfection really means.

Becoming Whole

Warning: we are about to go deep. I want you to know that I have studied this topic consistently for the past twenty years. I believe that we can become perfect. I also believe that if we are to reach our true potential, we must become perfect. It is within our power to lift ourselves up to being our very best.

The way to perfection is not a well-marked path, nor is it found among the teachings of man. In fact, man wants us to believe that no matter how hard we reach for it, we can never achieve it. The belief that perfection is an unattainable goal prevents us from understanding our true identity.

Plain and simple, you and I are children of God. As the French philosopher Teilhard de Chardin once said, "We are not human beings having a spiritual experience, we are spiritual beings having a human experience." Just like the tiny acorn seed, which holds within it all of the genetic information it needs to become a mighty oak tree, you and I possess the genetic makeup to become perfected beings.

The path to perfection requires us to develop spiritual intelligence. The teachings of perfection and the methods for developing spiritual intelligence are found within the sacred writings we commonly call scripture. Many deem them to be outdated, old-fashioned, and irrelevant, even though they have never studied them. Those who are seeking perfection must carefully consider them before they judge them likewise.

Be Ye Therefore Perfect

The greatest treatise on perfection is found in the fifth Chapter of Matthew in the New Testament. The fact that this discourse was delivered by Jesus must not dissuade those of you who are not Christians from studying it. Truth emanates from many different sources. Regardless of your religious persuasions, this dissertation is relevant to the pursuit of perfection. I invite you to study this text with an open mind.

I would especially like to draw your attention to verse forty-eight of this chapter. In it, we are told:

> Be ye therefore perfect, even as your father in heaven is perfect.

In urging us to be perfect, Jesus was not taunting us or teasing us. He was inviting us to take things to the next level, so he shared with us a powerful truth about our possibilities and about our potential. It is a truth almost too stunning to contemplate, and that is because you and I believe that perfection means to be entirely without any flaws, defects, or shortcomings.

The Telios Experience

Upon careful review of the original Greek manuscript, we find that the word "perfect" in the New Testament is actually translated from the Greek word "telios." This word does not mean to be without flaw; it simply means to become complete, finished, or fully developed. In other words, perfection is a process. It requires us to seek growth for the purpose of growing whole.

The flaws that make up our character and the mistakes we make along the way actually lend themselves to the process of perfection. They are the teaching moments that help us to see things as they really are. Without them, we would not progress.

Plain and Simple

Another clue about perfection comes to us from the twenty-seventh verse of the twenty-fifth Chapter of Genesis. The English translation describes Jacob as being plain. When we review the Hebrew text, we find that the word translated as "plain" is actually the Hebrew combination of "ish tam," which more correctly means whole, complete, perfect, and simple.

The adjective "plain" did not mean that Jacob was boring or without personality. Instead, it actually ascribed to him the same characteristics that are associated with the Greek word "telios."

This understanding helps us establish more concretely that perfection is a process and not necessarily an end state. He lived a plain life, not an extraordinary life, signifying that perfection is attainable by all. Living such a life actually made him extraordinary because he learned to become complete and whole. He became his very best. We must do the same. Our journey begins with a belief that we can reach for it.

More Grist for the Mill

The Bhagavad-Gita, a sacred text held by the Hindus in the same regard as the Judeo-Christian world considers the Bible, teaches that the goal of the Hindu disciple is to become perfect. The word "perfect" is derived from the word "arya."

In its most fundamental sense, "arya" means an effort or an uprising and overcoming. It is a path that must be chosen voluntarily, and it requires a personal battle or struggle. Those who choose this path must climb from level to level without fear. They must not shrink from the greatness of the task. Instead, they must press forward with courage, believing that there is no greatness that is unattainable.

The pathways of perfection followed by the "Aryan" require the denial of any and all external and internal influences that would prevent forward motion. One sees the attractions and distraction of the world, but chooses to become free from all enslaving passions. Perfection may only be attained by those who know how to seek and choose. The truth must be sought in everything.

Self-perfection is the aim. For this reason, only that which will ennoble and fulfill is pursued. When it is attained, it is poured out in work, love, joy, and knowledge upon the world.

Perfect Mindfulness

The pinnacle teaching of Buddhism is the belief that our moments of total awareness enlighten our pathways to perfection. The ultimate insight is the discovery that the way of attaining perfection is a path that we must walk many times. Each time, we begin anew. It is understood that the state of perfection may never be reached, but that does not inhibit us from becoming perfected because the process is the refiner's fire.

Perfection comes from constantly setting new standards and picking ourselves up when we fall short. It comes to us through a constant emphasis on forward progress. We often refer to it as continuous improvement, but in the grand scheme of things, it is referred to more correctly as eternal progression.

Only those who walk with purpose are capable of developing it. They will not be found running for the sake of speed, but rather they will be guided by true principles that lead them to a clear understanding of who they are and how they can make the world a better place.

I recognize that this discussion is somewhat mind-boggling. It is this way because we have set our sights too low for too long. Spiritual intelligence is rarely attained by watching TV, going to the movies, or playing video games. If you really want to know how the universe works, you must study the sacred writings of the world.

They all confirm that we are capable of becoming perfected beings. Perfection comes from eschewing the paths of darkness and walking in the light. The call of perfection is a simple call. It simply bids us to stand a little taller each day, so that we can become whole, complete, and fully finished. What a vibrant and evocative promise.

Hearing Your Voice

I am aware of my inability to communicate effectively the process of perfection. This awareness does not trouble me, because I understand that these are truths that must be discovered individually. The next level does not come by someone showing you the way. You must find it yourself. My desire is to simply expose the trailhead.

The work of understanding and receiving these truths now belongs to you. In order for you to fully value this chapter, you must study these concepts for yourself.

Don't be afraid of the truth. It may be found in many different sources, as illustrated in this chapter. The following questions and exercises are only meant to serve as guides on your journey. May they inspire in you a greater understanding of your true potential. Greatness is constantly hungering and thirsting to be whole.

What motivates you to reach for the next level?

_____

_____

_____

Do you believe continuous improvement is possible?

_____

_____

_____

How do you define perfection? Do you believe it is an attainable goal?

_____

_____

_____

_____

How do you create the energy you need to sustain forward progress?

_____

_____

_____

The development of spiritual intelligence creates a heightened state of consciousness that gently leads one to understand true potential and identity.

How do you develop spiritual intelligence?

_____

_____

_____

Define your next-level goal. Think about the strengths that you will need to reach for it and the obstacles that will get in your way. Create a plan that will harness your strengths and render the obstacles irrelevant.

What is your goal?

_____

_____

_____

What are your strengths?

_____

_____

_____

What are the obstacles?

_____

_____

_____

How will you get to the next level?

_____

_____

_____

What can you do to stand a little taller today?

_____

_____

_____

You are the only one who can define your limitations. Richard Bach raised a lot of eyebrows when he said:

> *"There is such a thing as perfection...and our purpose for living is to find that perfection and show it forth.... Each of us is in truth an unlimited idea of freedom. Everything that limits us we have to put aside."*

9

Objective Experts

Right now, I hope you are thinking "Perfection sounds more possible than ever." If you are feeling this way, please keep in mind that it is only possible when we pursue it as a process and not as an end state.

This is not always easy to remember, because we are so attached to the idea that perfection equals flawlessness. The work we must do to consistently reach for the next level is dependent upon our ability to embrace the concept of perfection as a completing process. Perfection is to be mindful of our highest potential and to allow continuous improvement to guide our forward progress.

Consider again the idea of the "last five pounds." Have you ever been that close? Were you fortunate enough to hit your goal weight? If you did, then you were perfect in that moment with regards to your weight loss efforts. The goal was completed.

Since weight loss can be defined quantitatively, it is easy to comprehend this example. We understand movement, whether up or down, in numbers, percentages, sizes, and volumes. As a result, we tend to gravitate towards goals that can be measured this way. We believe that we can reach these targets. We get more value from them because they are more easily measured. This standard serves us well when we are improving our competencies.

Measuring Behavior

Successful people realize that the next level can only be attained by an improvement in their behavior. Behavior-based improvement is rarely, if ever, able to be expressed in quantitative terms. This is because it is best measured by the experiences of those who are subject to the behavior we are seeking to grow.

Improvement, or the lack thereof, is demonstrated by the way they feel when they consider the person and his/her ability to behave in the desired way. To assess behavioral qualities, we cannot rely on the same scales we use to measure the quantities of our competencies. They are not able to give us the information we need to truly understand what is going on around us.

Some think that if we ask the right questions, we can measure anything, including improvement of behavior. Fascinating scales are then created to determine if key stakeholders agree or disagree that the person possesses and demonstrates the desired behavior. These scales give us some information, but they are not capable of really showing us the whole picture.

In addition, rating these scales honestly is a difficult process. A lot of people feel nervous about saying how they really feel. Their concern is that they will be identified and challenged for what they say. Still others see it as a way to exact vengeance for previous wrongs committed against them. As a result, they either rate too lightly or too harshly, making it very difficult to really interpret what is going on.

Behaviors can only be measured by qualitative means. It is true that, like physical growth, the behaviors of an individual develop over time, but we can't measure someone's listening skills with the same scale we employ to measure their height.

Understanding the quality of our relationships is much more meaningful than understanding the quantities of our results. To assess behavior, we must discover what others are feeling when they interact with us. This information sometimes startles us and may even throw us into a defensive posture, but we really are unable to grow without carefully considering what is being said.

Successful people know how to create and implement dynamic action plans, but the real challenge here is in developing a measuring tool. How do we measure feelings, attitudes, commitments, and perceptions? More importantly, how do we do this without being subject to the very elements (our feelings and thoughts) that identify the qualities we are seeking to measure? Can we really trust that we are getting better just because it feels like we are getting better? Of course not!

The statements others make are the chief indicators of our behavioral growth. We do not need to measure them, because they are the measurement.

What we really need is to interpret them, but that is hard to do on our own, because our individual biases and defensive postures often get in the way. Enrolling an objective set of eyes and ears helps accelerate our ability to move to the next level. It gives us a chance to see what is necessary to step out of where we are and into where we want to be.

Professional Help

Ok, admit it. The first thing that came into your mind when you read the term "professional help" was, "I don't need that; I am a successful person." I understand that this term evokes the thought of psychotherapy, but I am not worried about conjuring up that image, especially when we consider that the purpose of psychotherapy is to bring its benefactors to wholeness.

But go ahead and relax; this is not a prescription for psychotherapy. I am simply stating that if you want to go to the next level, you need help from people who are already there and maybe even people who are two or three levels up. They know the way.

As mentioned earlier, enrolling your stakeholders to help you improve is a critical part of the process, but let's face it: they are busy worrying about their own issues and they are far too influenced by your behaviors to give you consistent, positive, relative, and objective feedback. They are the experts on how they are feeling and what they are seeing, but they may have a difficult time telling you what you can do to improve. They know it when they see it; they just find it hard and odd to describe it to you in advance.

Those seriously pursuing the next level understand this. They know that they need additional help, even expert help, to quicken the rate of their growth.

To get it, they must look outside their normal circles of influence. They need a giant upon whose shoulders they can stand to gain a better perspective so that they can chart the right course.

As we grow, our susceptibility to different types of help grows too. There are three levels of professional help that I wish to bring more fully into your consciousness. I am sure you have heard the terms "mentor," "coach," and "sage." These labels are familiar, but the purposes of each are often blended and confused.

All three of these guides can assist you in interpreting your feedback, but they do it differently. The one you need depends on your position, your goal, and your level of maturity. It is just as natural to progress from one level to the next as it is to return to utilize the services of one again. In other words, though you may progress from one level to the next, it need not always be a linear process.

I have personally benefited from the help of all three. Here is how I see their role in the development of next-level behaviors.

The Mentor

A mentor is often in a position that you would like to be in and is generally willing and able to help you climb to the next level. They generally see themselves as a model for success and have a desire to mold their protégés into their own image. They hold up their successes and say, "If you want to be successful, follow this path." They are a great resource.

The fact that they want you to be like them is not a bad thing, as long as you are comfortable with the image into which you are being molded. You also want to make sure that you are the one picking the person who will be your mentor.

At different times in my career, I have benefitted immensely from the help of mentors. Leveraging their experiences helped me shorten my own learning curve.

We spent regular time together, which usually consisted of long lunches and time after hours in their offices. Their wisdom and their willingness to help me gave me the confidence I needed to reach for the next level.

One of my mentors regularly invited me to attend appointments with him. He taught me to intently observe what went on in each appointment. He asked me not to think about what I would say, but just to think about what I was hearing. We spent most of our time in the car, as we rode to and from those appointments, talking about what was going on with each customer and what happened in the customer visits. Those experiences were extremely valuable. I learned so much.

After a while, though, I began to experience a bit of an identity crisis. I was trying too hard to be like my mentor, and I forgot what it was like to be like the real me. When we discussed this, we agreed that it was time for him to kick me out of the proverbial nest. He told me that he had taught me everything that he could teach me and that it was now time for me to spread my own wings and find my own voice. His counsel in those moments demonstrated the love that a mentor develops for the protégé.

Knowing when it is time to transition from the mentor/protégé relationship is something successful mentors understand. It is also something that the successful protégé needs to understand. Some are tempted to hang on and maintain the relationship long after its point of value has passed.

A mentor can help assess strengths and weaknesses. They are also very good at helping others develop the skills and competencies they need for success. They are generally best at guiding the person who is just starting out on a new path.

When they are just starting out, success-minded people understand that they need help, and they are usually more than willing to work with a mentor. They frequently seek the help of senior individuals who model the competencies and behaviors they are trying to develop. They are willing to listen to the mentor's voice because they believe it will help them get to where they want to be faster than they can on their own.

The Coach

Coaching is an invaluable tool. Many leaders being coached value this service so much that they say they plan to continue being coached for a very long time. They see it as a way for their organizations to value them.

A coach is a personal and professional trainer whose efforts are focused on optimizing an individual's ability to develop the critical skills, competencies, and behaviors needed to advance in his/her career.

Coaching may be delivered via telephone and email, but the most effective format is when it is performed in regular, face-to-face meetings. Unlike the mentor, who holds up a picture of previous successes, the coach holds up a mirror, asks the clients to see their true potential, and then helps them reach for the next level.

The coach is commonly seen as an objective listener, capable of soliciting and giving real-time feedback. They seek to quickly build relationships of confidence and trust so that they can help the client see what he or she is unable to see.

A coach works to help the clients they serve capitalize on their strengths so that they can render their weaknesses irrelevant. They facilitate growth by creating personalized training.

They see things better than most, because they possess significant listening and observational skills. The good ones also have an ability to immerse themselves into the client's organizational culture without becoming biased by it. This means that they can act as a neutral, two-way conduit of information.

A coach is generally more involved than a mentor. Whereas the meetings with a mentor normally take place outside of the workplace, coaches generally prefer to meet inside of the system so that they can use their listening and observational skills to gain a perspective on the big picture.

The relationship between the coach and the coaching client is very important. If the trust is not there, it does not work. It is very important to select a coach who can challenge without reproving, because the challenges are what create the growth.

A commitment to the coaching relationship from both the coach and the client is extremely important. The growth facilitated by coaching does not happen overnight. It is important to begin the relationship with a commitment to working together for at least one year. The longer the two work together, the more effective the relationship becomes.

A good coach knows when it is time to transition the relationship and begins to prepare the leader, in advance, for the eventual separation.

I had lunch with a friend the other day, and he reminded me of the importance of this concept. He has two sons who enjoy playing baseball, and he coached both of them during their early years. When his oldest turned ten, he sent him on to a new coach. I asked him why, and he said because he had taught him everything he knew and it was time for him to move on to a more experienced coach so he could grow and improve.

Successful individuals, those that rise to the top of their organizations, often outgrow the abilities of their coach. This does not mean they should give up on coaching; it just means that it may be time to find a new coach.

The higher individuals climb, the harder it becomes to find someone who can coach, or who is willing to coach, them to the next level.

The Sage

Sages are known for their wisdom, calm judgment, and extensive experience. They help those around them to see things as they really are. They bring harmony to both life and leadership responsibilities.

They call their clients friends, and they love them enough to be completely and wholly honest. Their focus encompasses the personal and professional realms. Sages help their friends become anxiously engaged in the meaningful work of creating a legacy.

They foster deep and immediate trust, and this allows them to speak the most difficult truth without evoking defensiveness. Their contact is regular enough to be meaningful and infrequent enough to allow the space to ponder and comprehend. They form relationships that are much deeper and more intimate than those formed in the other professional relationships described in this chapter.

A sage is experienced enough to know the answer to most questions faced by their friends, but secure enough to only facilitate discovery. The sage recognizes that questions are more capable of accelerating growth than answers, and so they teach their friends how to ask powerful questions and invite them to ponder and search for their own answers. The sage is only interested in this objective and wants the friend to trust and rely on his/her own agenda.

The sage empowers interdependence, believing that it fosters the opportunity for others to contribute their strengths. Collaboration is a habit that is practiced regularly, not just a buzzword.

They give counsel when asked, without any expectation that it will be followed. This is because they want their friends to learn how to listen to their own voices. The sage's goal is to accelerate growth to the next level. They trust their friends to know how to use the information they share for their own best interest.

A true sage is one of the leader's most valuable resources. The relationship with the sage is not governed by time. It is governed by direction.

Sages possess a special talent for consulting leaders who are working on the "last five pounds." They teach the elimination of the non-essentials that rob the productive moments. They know how to bring focus to the things that matter most. They seek to expose that which matters least without making the friend feel judged or unworthy. Their constant upward focus calls their friends to soar in ascending spirals.

Hearing Your Voice

As a leader, you must learn how to seek the help that will foster your own voice instead of drown it out. This means that you need to learn how to set the proper boundaries in the mentoring, coaching and sageing relationships.

What are the nonessential things that clutter your days and steal your time?

_____

_____

_____

What are the habits you may have developed that do not serve a useful purpose?

_____

_____

_____

What are the things not started or unfinished that could add vigor, meaning, and joy to your life?

_____

_____

_____

Whom do you allow to speak into your life?

_____

_____

_____

How well do they foster your ability to listen to your own voice?

_____

_____

_____

How well do they focus you on positive outcomes?

_____

_____

_____

Think about the behaviors that you need to develop. Look deeply and think about where you are in relation to your goals. Now consider the descriptions in this chapter of the mentor, coach, and sage.

In what ways do you need to be mentored, coached, or saged?

_____

_____

_____

Are you willing to let someone help you see what you can't see so that you can become who you must become?

_____

_____

_____

_____

If you really want to go to the next level, then you must be willing to get the help you need. This is how you uncover your blind spots so that you may become your best.

The leader of the past was a person who knew how to tell. The leader of the future will be a person who knows how to ask.

Peter Drucker

10

The Final Ascent

I enjoy backpacking with my sons. In the summer months, we like to find the most difficult and challenging mountain peaks to ascend. We look forward to the miles of beauty and the elevating paths.

When we leave our car, we are full of energy and excited to get on the trail. The peak of choice stands in the distance, beckoning us onward. The top is always a long way from the trailhead, but it seems like it is close enough to touch.

Most of the trails we hike begin with either a minor descent or a relatively level segment. This portion of the trail gives us time to acclimate ourselves for the journey ahead. The easy and gradual beginning often lulls us into believing that the way ahead will be similar in kind.

As we march forward, the trail steepens. The closer we get to the top, the harder it becomes. The last thousand feet or so are always the most difficult on both body and mind.

False summits and switchback trails almost always get the best of us. There is always a point, not far from the top, when we wonder if we can do it and if it is really worth it. Sometimes the steepness of the path frightens us into wanting to turn back, but we always continue on.

There Are No Shortcuts

We usually wish for shortcuts, but realize that there are none. The final ascent must always be conquered. It is where we prove whether or not we really want to make it to the top. We always run into people who decided they could not make the top.

The journey to the next level is similarly designed. Many join the journey at the trailhead, but only the very best continue to the top. The toughest times on the trail remind us that it takes work to become a finisher.

Today, hardly anybody is willing to wait for anything. Our world demands speed. We have fast food, one-minute managers, fast passes, and many other expressions that call for quickness. Who has time for the daily grind of continuous improvement? We say we want it, but are we really committed to having it?

Those who want to go to the next level understand that they are going to have to do the work to get it. It is not enough to want it. That is only the beginning. They must stretch every day. They must plan the day with the thought in mind that the work they do today will be the first and next steps to reaching their goal. Anything else will divert their focus and make the road much more difficult.

The Finish Line

Many of the characters searching for the name of the tree in *The Tale of the Name of the Tree* got close to delivering, but only one crossed the finish line. There is a great sense of accomplishment that comes from finishing what we start. Successful people are finishers. They rarely start something that they are not willing to finish.

Fortunately, finishing is a behavior that can be learned. While there are many steps that create this behavior, five steps seem to be the most critical. These steps don't just help us finish what we start; they also keep us anxiously engaged in forward progress.

Step 1 - See Yourself Finishing

This is where it begins. If you can't see yourself crossing the finish line, then you may as well never begin. We can dream about many different things, but finishers know they can finish before they ever begin. They don't pursue things that they cannot finish.

This is a critical step. When we begin with the end in mind, we can see what it will take for us to finish. With this vision in mind, we are able to keep going when things become difficult. In those moments, we can rely on the vision of finishing to push through the challenging moments.

Step 2 - Practice, Practice, Practice

I have known many people who decided that they wanted to be a certain way and thought that just because they said it, they would become it. They think the secret is wanting something badly enough. Rarely, if ever, do we get what we want just because we want it. We must be willing to exert ourselves over and over again if we want to become a finisher.

Our first awareness of those we consider extraordinary usually comes when we see them crossing the finish line. We don't see all the hours of practice they put in to get to the next level. Those who become great are constantly practicing. They work harder and longer than anybody else. That is how they get ahead. It is not easy to get up earlier than anybody else, but that is usually what it takes. Henry Wadsworth Longfellow said it best:

The heights by great men reached and kept, were not obtained by sudden flight. But they, while their companions slept, were toiling upward in the night.

To be a finisher, you must be willing to do what others are unwilling to do.

Step 3 - Adversity Is Part of the Deal

It will not be easy. Along the way to finishing, you will be tested. You must prove to yourself and others that you really want to finish. The hardest part will always be the final ascent, but there are other challenges along the way.

The period of stretching and adjusting that comes in the beginning makes the start also one of the most difficult periods.

At the beginning, usually it is self-doubt that makes us wonder if we have what it takes. At the end, it is fatigue that tries to discourage us. Don't ever let doubt or fatigue stop you from finishing. Just keep at it, and you will be refreshed.

The struggles along the way are of equal value. They join together to make the finish line sweet. Just stick with it, and remember that adversity is part of the deal.

Step 4 - Find Those Who Will Cheer You On

Successful people usually hear the criticism of the world and rarely hear the praise. This is a mistake. If you really want to finish, you must realize that you cannot do it by yourself. You really do need the support and help of those who are here to cheer you on.

I like to enter endurance events. There are always people along the way who are only there to cheer and serve those in the race. I don't think I would have finished any of my races without the help of these kind people. They have the power to lift me up in my most trying times by simply speaking an encouraging word or giving me a glass of water.

Running past this aid or closing my ears to their encouraging voices would be a serious mistake. To be a finisher, we need the support of others.

Step 5 - Find Joy in the Journey

Crossing the finish line is definitely one of my favorite moments, but I realize that it is only a moment. I enjoy it—it brings things to a close. But I know that the real joy comes from all of the lessons that I have learned along the way.

The moments that lead up to finishing are what make the finish something worth noting. If we were just able to cross finish lines every day without any of the preparation, adversity, or help from others along the way, it would be meaningless. These are the real reasons finishing strong is so fulfilling—because along the way we have stretched ourselves in ways we could not have previously imagined.

Raising the Bar

Some people see finish lines as the end. Those reaching for the next level see them as a new beginning. In the flash of a moment, they become the baseline for their future aspirations. This is why they like finishing so much. They understand that finish lines crossed become the inspiration and motivation to reach for new heights. Once crossed, they become the next starting line.

Hearing Your Own Voice

Finish lines help us re-ignite our passion for living. They give us the sense of accomplishment that we need in order to move on. When we acknowledge our finish lines, we are ready to move on to new starting lines.

What finish lines are you crossing right now?

_____

_____

_____

How are they preparing you for the future?

_____

_____

_____

Think about the finish lines you recently crossed. Consider the lessons you learned at the starting line, during the trek, and at the finish line. Think about the people that supported you along the way.

Describe your heroic moments, the ones when you felt yourself moving to the next level. Capture your thoughts here before you move on to the next chapter. Write down the valuable lessons you learned. How will those lessons serve as baseline behaviors for your next adventure?

_____

_____

_____

What finish lines have you always wanted to cross but, for some reason or another, have not yet crossed?

_____

_____

_____

What inspires you to go for it when the goal is in sight but your energy levels are low?

_____

_____

_____

What strengths do you rely on to pick you up?

_____

_____

The time now belongs to you. It is your time, and you are a finisher. I am cheering you on. Be a finisher!

Stick to your plan, until it sticks to you. Beginners are many, but finishers are few.

Anonymous

11

Back to the Tree

Let's face it, reaching for the next level is meaningless if we do not know why we are doing it. If we really expect to become finished and fully developed, then our journeys must be connected to something meaningful, even something bigger than ourselves. Without the right purpose, we can't even hang on, let alone cross the finish line.

The majority of the characters in the *Tale of the Name of the Tree* found this out for themselves. Though each one was hungry, they were unable to make it back without forgetting the name of the tree. We know their story, the details of what happened to them along the way, but you and I know that what happens to us is generally not the source of our problems; it is merely the result of them.

Our purpose in reaching for the next level must be to use the gifts and talents we learned at our previous levels to bless and nourish the lives of others. It must not ever be a selfish pursuit, or our enlightened moments will certainly be overcome by darkness. When the name of the tree was spoken, the fruit fell for all of the animals, not just the Tortoise and his family.

I truly believe that enlightened beings, those constantly reaching for the next level, are not meant to silently travel by themselves. If they truly want to enjoy what they are gaining, they must be willing to share what they have with the rest of us. Our inability to make this choice generally results in the stumbles so perfectly demonstrated by those who were found running back to the tree for their own personal gain. They never realized the potential given to them by the Great Chief over the Mountains. Instead, they lost their gift along the way.

Material Gains Are Not the Source of Happiness

I was once closely associated with a very successful man. His many achievements were the emblems of his success. He enjoyed the finer things in life and travelled the world in first-class cabins.

One day, we were having a conversation. My wife and I had recently moved into a new home, which resulted in a pretty major commute to the office. I told him that I was worried about the miles I was putting on my car. He said that he was worried about the miles that I was putting on myself.

Our new home was beautiful, and we were living in a wonderful area. I considered his concern, and then I told him that we were much happier. He then said something that completely surprised me. He said, "I wouldn't know anything about that; I have never been happy."

Here was a man who had the best of everything, yet he said that he had never been happy. Since that time, I have met many successful people who feel the same way. It is not really that they are unhappy; they just know they are missing something. They know that there is something more. They have the dream car, the dream house, and the dream life, but they are often longing for something more. They can't help but think, "Is this all there really is?"

Of course, there is something more, but we cannot find what we are naturally looking for by achieving more. Our achievements will never fill us up. They can only be, and were only ever meant to be, a part of what it takes to fill us up. They make up many of the foundational experiences that motivate us to move to the next level, but they can only take us so far.

Giving Back

Sometimes, we forget that we live in abundance. We hold on to what we have with clenched fists instead of open hands. Our attention is so firmly fixed on achieving more that we forget to look around to discover how we can create more meaning.

Meaningful experiences come when we serve and help others. We cannot enjoy the fruit by ourselves. When it is ready to be harvested, we must share it with those around us, or else it will rot and decay.

Our ability to grow and develop is dependent upon our willingness to share our successes with others. There is usually some sort of significant movement to force our most successful individuals to give of their resources. We must not wait to be compelled to give in meaningful ways. When we are, our freedom is violated, and we lose the meaning that comes from voluntarily giving from our own heart.

Our successes are to be shared via acts of free will. It is the only way that we can truly make them meaningful. Next-level living requires us to be consistently thinking and acting in ways that create opportunities for others to also reach for their next level. We will not enjoy our successes until we see that they are given to us so that we can help others succeed.

Leaving a Legacy

The journey to the next level is about establishing and securing a lasting legacy. This great work is an everyday commitment. It is not something that we can wait until our final days are upon us to do. It is the process of discovering who we are. Early in our adult life, we are necessarily focused on what we do, but this must not remain our focus as we age. Instead, we must learn to focus on who we are.

As our careers become established and stable, the questions that move us to the next level become more obvious. We think about these questions often, yet for some reason we tell ourselves that we will answer them "some other day."

Unfortunately, "some other day" rarely ever comes, and "legacy making" continues to be a topic only occasionally found in our daily conversations. Our supply of tomorrows eventually runs out without us giving it the proper consideration it deserves.

Shaping our legacy requires us to make meaning out of our lives. The questions we ask are the fuel for that process. The more powerful the question, the more clearly we can see who we are and who we may become.

Simple Truths

I regularly visit with individuals who are nearing the end of their lives. One of the questions I like to ask during my time with these wise individuals is, "What is the most important lesson you have learned during your life?" Their responses to this question are amazingly similar. Here are the five most common answers I hear:

1. *The Simple Things Matter Most*
2. Humor and Time Cure Most Pains
3. Service to Others Is the Most Satisfying Activity

4. Choose Your Spouse Carefully - It Will Be Your Most Important Decision
5. Work Hard in a Field and Role You Enjoy

There they are, the secrets of life. Do any of them surprise you? I wonder if we fully appreciate the valuable wisdom that is found in these simple declarations of those who will soon cross the finish line of life. If we do, we will build our lives around them.

These are the answers, and we have permission to use them. If a teacher gave you the answers to an important test, and also gave you permission to use those answers on the test, would you ignore them? Of course not! That would be ridiculous. You would use them to your advantage.

Now Is the Time

No matter how old you are, today is the best day to study these answers and to begin ordering your life around them. Real opportunities to move to the next level happen every day. We miss many of them because we are so caught up in serving those things that matter least at the expense of the things that matter most.

It doesn't have to be that way. The journey to the next level is accelerated when we willingly ask ourselves two simple questions each and every day. The questions are simple, but to get the answers, we must create the space to think deeply.

Here are the questions:

"What do I really, really, really, want out of life?"
and
"What do I need to do today to get that?"

The time you spend pondering your answers to these simple questions will help you shape who you want to become.

At first, these questions will be difficult to answer. That is because we don't spend enough time thinking about these questions. Your answers will come easier as you think about them every day. It is the best way to discover what your next level will be. It is the best way to establish your legacy. Don't wait for the crisis that will always come. Live today! Love today! It is the only way to be.

Hearing Your Voice

Let's go back to the beginning, even to the most important question for you to figure out. It is critical because you can't help or serve anybody else until you know the answer. Please hear the following questions in your own voice. Say them out loud and really think about your answers.

Who am I?

_____

_____

_____

How will I be remembered?

_____

_____

_____

How can I become whole?

_____

_____

_____

What will my legacy be?

_____

_____

_____

Think about the people in your sphere of influence. Consider their successes and their strengths. Now think about how you can help them reach for their next level. Think about how you can serve them.

Write down the names of the people that you will help. Write down how you will help them.

Now call them up and tell them that you were thinking about them and that you would like to offer your help. Be ready: some may not want your help, so don't force it. Others may want you to help them differently than the way you envisioned. Either way, there is an opportunity to add value. Just continue to reach out, and you will begin to create a legacy that lasts.

Our actions, the way we serve others, and the way we reach for the next level are the footprints we leave behind for our posterity to examine and celebrate. Be there!

If something comes to life in others because of you, then you have made an approach to immortality.

Norman Cousins

Author's Notes

Defining Moments - Andrew Thorn - The Authentic Me

When I was a kid, my dad often told me, "People don't care how much you know until they know how much you care." I know now that he was quoting Teddy Roosevelt, but when I was growing up, I thought these were his words.

He certainly lived by them. He seemed to know and care about everyone. I recall driving through many of the towns that surrounded our area and him pointing to businesses and houses and then telling the story of the people who worked and lived there.

I remember sitting at malls or airports with my dad and just watching the people as they would walk past. We would rarely comment; we just sat and studied them. I learned a lot about expressions and emotions during those frenetic moments. I wanted to be like him, so I began to care more about people than I cared about anything else.

My dad wasn't the only one who enjoyed and cared about people. My mother also spent a lot of time learning about the nature of individuals.

During my early teens Mom was given an assignment from our church to be the Cultural Refinement Leader. This was an amazing opportunity for our family. Each month, she was responsible for learning about a different culture and presenting what she learned in the form of a one-hour lesson to the other ladies in our local congregation.

To prepare for her class, she would practice her lessons on us. I was fascinated by the different cultures, beliefs, and values that she was discovering. Sometimes, she would even invite people from these cultures to have dinner and spend the evening in our home. These experiences taught me to embrace the beauties of diversity. As a result, I learned to see other groups through the eyes of discovery and wonder.

The Joy of Work

My mother also taught me how to work hard. At four years old, I began to receive chores that were specifically assigned for me to do each day. She was great at following up, and I learned that it was better to meet or exceed her standards than it was to not get the chores done. I worked at something every day, and when I got good at doing it, I was given a new assignment, something that was just a little bit harder and that would test me. I don't remember ever living at home without a regular chore that was specifically assigned to me.

At twelve years old, I began my first real job throwing papers for the Whittier Daily News. In addition to delivering the paper, I was also responsible for collecting the monthly subscription fees. At least once a month, I visited each home and asked the subscriber to pay his or her bill.

I quickly learned that if I provided good service, it was easier to get paid when collection time came around. I applied my dad's formula and did my best to care for each customer. I routinely asked them to tell me where they wanted their paper to be delivered. I held many jobs during my teenage years. More than any of the others, this one taught me how to listen to what the customer wanted and needed.

A Different Kind of Work

At nineteen years old, I embarked on a two-year service mission for my church. I was assigned to serve in Maracaibo, Venezuela and the surrounding areas. I learned to speak fluent Spanish, and, in my heart, I became a Venezuelan.

I learned many things from this pivotal experience (i.e., what it means to be a foreigner, the importance of service, the importance of working as a team, and how to harness my individual initiative).

It was an exhilarating time; through it, I refined my ability to care about the people I worked with in order to build intimate relationships of confidence and trust. I truly learned to love the people of Venezuela. That foundation continues to make it easy for me to express this type of love in all aspects of my life.

Two Become One – And Then Nine

In the spring of 1988, I met Stacy Van Liew. Our love grew quickly, and we were married in August of that year.

Describing the magic of our life together sounds unreal. From the very beginning, Stacy saw in me more than I saw in myself. Her commitment to supporting me in every dream, regardless of how crazy it sounds, is amazing. I could never be who I am without her by my side. She inspires me to be a better me. There is no doubt in my mind that she is the source of my energy and love for life. I am so thankful to be her husband.

Together, we are the parents of seven children. Our home is constantly filled with the sounds of life. We love them and enjoy supporting them in their many activities. They are beautiful individuals. The lessons we learn from them are too numerous to list here. Suffice it to say that they are the source of great meaning and joy.

Back to Work

Early in our married life, I went to work for my uncle. He owned a commercial finance company. My job was to help small business owners acquire the equipment they needed to run their operations. I spent my days discovering the current and future needs of the entrepreneurs in the Los Angeles area.

I enjoyed being a friend to my clients as much as being a source of business capital. I liked to listen to their challenges, their successes, and their dreams. I liked to encourage them. The longer I was in the business, the more I became known for something other than the money I was lending. My clients did business with me because I listened from a perspective that was external to their other circles. They quickly became comfortable sharing everything with me, and that is why I eventually left the world of lending financial capital for the world of developing human capital.

My Own Business

In 1995, I decided to leave my uncle's employ to start my own company. I was twenty-nine years old and sitting on the top of the world.

In March of that year, I founded Thalman Financial, Inc. It was an interesting move. I immediately discovered that there was a lot more to running a business than making sales. Each day brought a new lesson. Some were more painful than others.

The enterprise was successful, and it continued to grow at a steady rate. My biggest challenges came from leading my people. These challenges often consumed the majority of my day. At times, I felt like there was no way I could win.

I learned the importance of setting clear expectations. I also learned that it was my responsibility to communicate effectively. I couldn't just assume that my people understood what I was talking about. I had to follow-up frequently to make sure.

Back to School

I was hungry to become a better leader, so I frequently attended seminars on this topic. My attendance in these events made me want to learn even more.

In an attempt to quench my thirst for knowledge, I enrolled in Pepperdine's Executive MBA program. The program began with a semester on Organizational Behavior taught by Wayne Strom. The coursework was delivered through action-learning modules. I enjoyed the opportunity to work and learn with peers without the pressure of being a Leader with a capital "L."

Most of my classmates came from large organizations. I was one of the only entrepreneurs in our cohort, and this gave me an opportunity to learn and study with some very skilled and highly trained leaders.

The Healthy Me

During my MBA program, I began to focus on being healthy. I was still in my mid-thirties, but I could tell that age was taking its toll. I began walking, and then I started to run. Running led to cycling, and then I renewed my passion for swimming.

It seemed natural to put them all together, so I signed up for my first Ironman Triathlon in June of 2002.

Training and competing in that event taught me that I set the boundaries. I learned that if I want something bad enough, I can do it. There will always be some pain, but the joy of crossing the finish line makes it all worth it.

Tragedy Strikes

One morning, on my way to class, Stacy called with news that my father had passed away. I was only thirty-five years old when he died, and he was only sixty-five. I remember thinking that he was way too young to be leaving this life.

His death shocked me. It wasn't just that he was gone; the reality also sunk in that I was next in line. For the first time, I saw my own mortality. I knew that I was going to die. I looked at my children and tried to imagine them without a father. I looked at my life and asked myself if I was really doing the things I wanted to do and if what I was doing would actually make a difference. My answer was a resounding "no" on both accounts.

This reality check set in motion a significant period of growth in my life. I decided to change my life and my career. I wasn't happy with what I was doing. I knew that my life purpose was not aligned with that work. It was something I knew for a long time, but I was afraid to do anything about it.

The lifestyle my success provided made it difficult for me to walk away. I enjoyed my life, but I often felt like helping people incur debt was a waste of my time and talents. I wanted to help people become liberated, not encumbered. I wanted to discover the "authentic me," and I wanted to help others find their "authentic selves."

My father's death gave me the courage to let go. I decided to rid myself of the obligations associated with my business. I really did let it all go. At first, I worried that everyone would think I failed and that I had to go out of business. Eventually, I came to realize that it really didn't matter what anyone else thought. I was shedding a weight that was keeping me from reaching my potential, and it felt good. I felt really happy. I never looked back, and I can honestly say that I am being who I want to be and doing what I want to do.

Back to School Again

In August of 2002, I founded Telios Corporation. As mentioned in chapter 8, telios is a Greek word that means "complete, whole, and fully finished." This company became the vehicle for realizing my lifelong passion of evoking excellence in others.

I knew that I had much to learn, so shortly after the formation of this new company, I enrolled in a doctoral program in organizational psychology at The California School of Professional Psychology in San Diego. The campus is 147 miles from my home, which meant that I was in the car for more than four hours a day.

The sale of my company afforded me the luxury of being enrolled in a full-time program. I attended class Monday through Friday. All of my coursework was focused on individual development and the impact of the individual in organization and team settings.

The time away at school and on the road, combined with the energy and time needed to start a new business, added to the stress associated with completing a significant remodel of our home. To make matters even more interesting, Stacy was pregnant with of our sixth child and confined to bed for seven months. The entire package pushed the limits of my sanity.

Never, at any time, did I have to struggle so hard to live a balanced life. It was a constant challenge. Those experiences taught me so much about living in the present moment of mindfulness. I learned how to live a quality life in the midst of the constant demands of quantity. Life is still busy, but nowhere near as busy as it was during that time. The lessons I learned helped me understand how to always keep my life and leadership responsibilities in full harmony.

It took six years to become Dr. Andrew Thorn. When it was over, I felt like a new person. My core blossomed, and my capacity to listen, care, and facilitate grew to unexpected levels.

The Telios Experience

As I mentioned earlier, the death of my father made me profoundly aware of my own mortality. I knew that I was in the second half of life. The aging process was constantly on my mind.

Up until that point, my life was focused on achievement. My successes brought a lot of happiness, but they did not fill me up. That is why I knew that I needed to sell my financial company. I could not continue working in that venture without asking myself, "Is this all there really is?"

I realized that I needed to begin a transition from ambition to meaning. My ambition drove the first half of my life; now it was time to make sense of it all.

I enrolled several friends to help me create a program that would help me and others manage this transition. I began by calling it The Game of Life and later renamed it The Telios Experience. This process is a legacy-making exercise.

The Telios Experience is a living experience, and it continues to grow. We built a special table around which our groups meet. It was hand carved. Not a single power tool was used to carve it. Stacy and I recently purchased forty-six acres in Prescott, Arizona. We are now dreaming of the retreat that we will build. It is a place where those we work with can escape the pressures of their daily lives and focus on their legacies. I know many people will come and stay with us in the near future. They are coming. We just don't know their names yet.

Aspirations

I believe our aspirations are the permission we give ourselves to soar in ascending spirals. Our lives are full and balanced when we are living our dreams.

I recently played the part of Joseph in *Joseph and the Amazing Technicolor Dreamcoat*. It was a wonderful opportunity for me to live a dream. I worked hard to be in excellent shape and to sing and dance. These are skills that I knew I had, but that I had never developed before.

It was not easy to fit it into my busy schedule. I did it because I wanted to model what a full life looks like. I believe that if we want to have a balanced life, we must constantly push ourselves to new levels. We are created to be continuously improving. We only feel out of balance when we are resting or neglecting opportunities to develop our individual talents.

From this experience, I learned that the word "someday" generally robs us of the opportunities that shape us and form us. "Someday" rarely comes—it merely stands as a mirage of hope in our lives. Now is the time to be who we always wanted to be. I will never wait for someday again.

I am constantly examining the aspirations that I dream for my life. I hold them up so that I can see them in broad daylight. I know that if I want to fulfill them, I must identify the commitments that will make them real. Then I must determine if I am truly willing to live according to those commitments. This analysis focuses my time on the things that really matter most. As a result, I am constantly reaching to become my best.

Who Is Andrew Thorn?

I share this story of my defining moments with you so that you may begin to see me for who I really am. I want you to know who I am before we talk about what I do, and I want to know who you are too.

You may be wondering; "What does Andrew really do?" The answer is actually kind of simple.

Think for a moment of the most successful person you know. Now, imagine that person taking life to the next level. What would it take? Do you think that because the person is so successful, the thought of getting better rarely enters his or her mind? Or do you think the person is constantly trying to figure out how to be better? The successful people I know are usually focused on the latter. How hard do you think it is for them to get better?

My experience with successful people indicates that the closer one gets to greatness, the harder it is to move toward outstanding. It is extremely difficult to discover the miniscule changes required to raise the bar. Now, imagine what it takes for that person to grow from outstanding to extraordinary. Are you as excited by that prospect as I am?

That is the work that I do. I help highly successful people become their very best. I do it by listening to them so that I can discover who they really are. This makes it possible for me to speak the truth to them in ways that they have rarely ever heard it spoken to them before. Most have never had a friend like me. I love and care for them in ways that are difficult to describe, but they are real. The only way to truly understand it is to experience it.

My purpose is to help you enjoy life more by helping you understand the deeper level meaning of your successes. I am not concerned about helping you make more money or helping you achieve more. My goal is for you to become the best you possible so that you can enjoy more life.

Achieving more will not fill that gap. The only way to fill it is to focus on what matters most. That is what I help people do, and that is why I always say that I have the greatest job in the world.

Getting Involved

I believe that when I asked you to think of the most successful person you know, you probably thought of yourself. I know you understand the challenge of taking things to the next level. I am sure the thought of it excites and energizes you, just as it does me.

I deliver my services through a limited number of intense and intimate one-on-one or small group settings.

You can find out more about these activities by contacting me directly at 760-559-3548.

I look forward to meeting you and seeing the real you.

Live Today! Love Today!

Andrew
To Be Continued...

Enrollment Offer

Congratulations! You Are A Success!
Now What Is Your Next Move?

Andrew Thorn provides behavioral-based development strategies to individuals who are seeking to establish their legacies and bring their lives and leadership responsibilities into full harmony.

Founded in 2002, the company delivers its services to a limited number of highly successful senior leaders and private individuals who represent some of the largest publicly and privately held organizations in the world. Services are realized in one-on-one, executive team and small group settings.

Our approach is distinctive in two respects:

First, our "Aspire – Engage – Become" methodology is founded on timeless principles that drive authentic behavioral-based growth. Our clients are already very successful. Our process helps them discover how to reach for their next level.

Second, we understand that we are the catalyst and not the voice of the growth experience. Our clients learn to see things as they really are. They also learn to see who they really are. We facilitate their awareness; they are responsible for raising the bar.

Our services are designed to leverage the perspectives of key stakeholders, those who are in positions to witness key behaviors and comment on their impact.

We believe that asking the right questions leads to greater focus and clarity, which, in turn, creates the momentum for thriving individual development.

We Invite You to Engage Us in the Following Services:

- **Presencia™** - a series of intimate, one-on-one behavioral-based personal and professional development experiences

- **The Telios Experience™** - an intimate legacy-building exercise, bringing wholeness and balance to four critical life pursuits—relationships, spiritual intelligence, physical health, and professional development

- **Symphony™** - a dynamic way of accelerating the professional and personal development of emerging, high-potential and mid-level leaders, presented in corporate settings through our unique peer-to-peer methodology

- **Summit™** - a shared growth experience of individual leaders and small business owners who are similarly focused on becoming their very best, presented through a series of small and mid-size group settings

Capture the Hearts and Minds of Your Audience

Thank you for your interest in inviting Dr. Andrew Thorn to speak at your upcoming event. We know how important it is to find a speaker who is capable of capturing the minds and hearts of your audience. Andrew continually demonstrates that he is this type of speaker.

His presentations are regularly heard in the United States, Canada, Mexico, and South America.

His platforms range from conventions, to large corporate gatherings, to small group sessions. Audiences consistently proclaim him to be inspiring and energetic. Andrew is a "story teller." He believes in giving participants opportunities to ponder his materials before he begins his sessions and then giving them practical takeaways to use after his presentations are over.

Select keynotes by Dr. Andrew Thorn

1. Aspire: Permission to Soar in Ascending Spirals

Andrew energizes the room by leading a dialogue on the place of dreams in a grownup's life. We all dreamed wonderful dreams when we were children: why must that stop when we become adults? This keynote address will reconnect your audience with their individual dreams and teach them how to soar higher in their personal and professional lives. The magical idea of ascending spirals is discussed from the perspective of identifying strategies for maintaining forward progress. Andrew will discuss the importance of rest and how your audience can use it to get what they want. Practical stories from his one-on-one experiences with senior leaders help your group identify the commitments necessary to move from wishes to aspirations, from aspirations to commitments, and from commitments to results. He leaves one clear message: We All Have Permission to Soar in Ascending Spirals!

2. Engage: Living the Commitments That Accelerate Growth

Thriving individuals recognize that they are responsible for discovering, and ultimately living, the commitments that accelerate their growth. They also understand that growth does not happen by accident, but rather from a culmination of small, but meaningful steps that help focus short-term activity in areas that will produce long-term benefits. Andrew helps participants create balance between pleasure and meaning by asking questions like, "Will this activity make me happy?" and "Will the successful completion of this activity create a long-term, positive impact in my life?"

Engagement is the result of focusing our vision, creativity, innovation, and hard work on the things that matter most in our lives. Andrew discusses his renowned "Daily Question" process and the formula for creating the perfect day. He inspires the audience to see things as they really are so they can plan, prioritize, and schedule their lives in a way that will help them stay focused on the future while avoiding the countless pleasurable distractions that can lead to nowhere.

3. Become: Standing Whole and Ready to Lead with Purpose

Life is the greatest game we will ever play. It is a game that constantly changes, which makes it both frustrating and fascinating. It is a process of becoming. Too many people define themselves by what they do, believing people follow them because of their achievements. There is no doubt that our abilities are a vital part of our success, but they really only make a small contribution to our journey of becoming whole and leading with purpose.

In this presentation, Andrew introduces The BECOME Formula™, which focuses the audience on the pursuit of becoming. To become your best, you must be willing to see the best you. Here is the formula for BECOMING:

B – Believe that there is room to grow.
E – Envision your success.
C – Collect feedback from others.
O – Open up to being great.
M – Measure what success will take, and develop a plan.
E – Everyday, do something to move yourself closer to becoming your best self.

4. Who Do You Want to Be When You Grow Whole? Finding Meaning in the Second Half of Life

You've achieved so much in your life: success in business, a great lifestyle, financial security . . . yet something is missing. You are aging, and you are hungry to fulfill your lifelong aspirations. Time seems to be slipping away. The actions and things that brought purpose in the first half of your life no longer satisfy your desire to grow. You want to do what you want to do, but you feel constricted by the demands placed upon you. You are entering the second half of life, and all you hear about it is what you will lose as you age. But what will you gain? In this high-energy keynote address, Andrew shows you how to explore the fundamental principles of working (and living) with passion, purpose, and vitality—and he challenges you to step outside your comfort zone to rise above self-imposed limitations. If you are striving for new and extraordinary results in the second half of life, Andrew will help you discover the keys to growing *whole* instead of growing *old*.

Dr. Andrew Thorn is available on a limited basis.

Please call 1-800-561-8237 today to schedule him at your event.